Cambridge Elements

Elements in Corporate Governance
edited by
Thomas Clarke
UTS Business School, University of Technology Sydney

INNOVATION VERSUS FINANCIALIZATION IN THE US PHARMACEUTICAL INDUSTRY

Öner Tulum
The Academic-Industry Research Network

William Lazonick
The Academic-Industry Research Network

Shaftesbury Road, Cambridge CB2 8EA, United Kingdom

One Liberty Plaza, 20th Floor, New York, NY 10006, USA

477 Williamstown Road, Port Melbourne, VIC 3207, Australia

314–321, 3rd Floor, Plot 3, Splendor Forum, Jasola District Centre, New Delhi – 110025, India

103 Penang Road, #05–06/07, Visioncrest Commercial, Singapore 238467

Cambridge University Press is part of Cambridge University Press & Assessment, a department of the University of Cambridge.

We share the University's mission to contribute to society through the pursuit of education, learning and research at the highest international levels of excellence.

www.cambridge.org
Information on this title: www.cambridge.org/9781009707992

DOI: 10.1017/9781009708012

© Öner Tulum and William Lazonick 2025

This publication is in copyright. Subject to statutory exception and to the provisions of relevant collective licensing agreements, no reproduction of any part may take place without the written permission of Cambridge University Press & Assessment.

When citing this work, please include a reference to the DOI 10.1017/9781009708012

First published 2025

A catalogue record for this publication is available from the British Library

ISBN 978-1-009-70799-2 Hardback
ISBN 978-1-009-70798-5 Paperback
ISSN 2515-7175 (online)
ISSN 2515-7167 (print)

Cambridge University Press & Assessment has no responsibility for the persistence or accuracy of URLs for external or third-party internet websites referred to in this publication and does not guarantee that any content on such websites is, or will remain, accurate or appropriate.

For EU product safety concerns, contact us at Calle de José Abascal, 56, 1°, 28003 Madrid, Spain, or email eugpsr@cambridge.org

Innovation versus Financialization in the US Pharmaceutical Industry

Elements in Corporate Governance

DOI: 10.1017/9781009708012
First published online: September 2025

Öner Tulum
The Academic-Industry Research Network

William Lazonick
The Academic-Industry Research Network

Author for correspondence: Öner Tulum, onertulum@gmail.com

Abstract: Mandated by the Inflation Reduction Act of 2022, the US government is negotiating with pharmaceutical companies over the "maximum fair price" of ten drugs widely used by Medicare patients. The pharmaceutical companies contend that a "fair" price is a "value-based price" that enables their shareholders to capture the value the drug creates for society and warn that lowering drug prices will reduce investments in new drugs. This Element responds to these arguments by showing that pharmaceutical companies (a) should have their drug prices regulated, given scale economies in supplying drugs and price inelasticity of drug demand; (b) use their profits from unregulated drug prices to distribute cash dividends and stock buybacks to shareholders; (c) do not typically rely upon investment by shareholders to fund drug innovation; and (d) benefit from "collective and cumulative learning" in foundational and translational research that is antecedent and external to their investments in clinical research.

Keywords: Medicare drug price negotiations, accessible and affordable medicines, collective and cumulative learning, stock buybacks, shareholder-value ideology

© Öner Tulum and William Lazonick 2025

ISBNs: 9781009707992 (HB), 9781009707985 (PB), 9781009708012 (OC)
ISSNs: 2515-7175 (online), 2515-7167 (print)

Contents

1 High Drug Prices and the Inflation Reduction Act of 2022   1

2 What Is a "Fair" Drug Price?   7

3 Foundational, Translational, and Clinical Research   40

4 Collective and Cumulative Learning in Translational Research   47

5 The Knowledge Ecosystem of Drug Discovery and Development, and the Fair Price for a Drug   71

References   76

1 High Drug Prices and the Inflation Reduction Act of 2022

It is no secret that the cost of prescription drugs is out of control in the United States, a nation that, alone among the advanced economies, leaves price-setting to the pharmaceutical industry (including drug producers, prescription benefit managers, and health insurance companies). With the largest national market for pharmaceutical drugs, in 2022 the United States had 4.3 percent of the global population, but 43 percent of the world's $1.5 trillion in pharmaceutical drug revenues (Mikulic 2024). As displayed in Figure 1, with data centering on 2021, the United States had the highest annual drug spending per capita at $1,432, followed by Germany with $1,006, Japan with $829, and Canada with $814.

According to the US Department of Health and Human Services: "In 2022, U.S. prices across all drugs (brands and generics) were nearly 2.78 times as high as prices in the comparison countries. U.S. prices for brand drugs were at least 3.22 times as high as prices in the comparison countries, even after adjustments for estimated U.S. rebates" (HHS 2024). The passage of the Inflation Reduction Act (IRA) of 2022 marked a step forward toward prescription drug-price regulation in the United States. Among other things, the IRA authorized the Centers for Medicare & Medicaid Services (CMS) to embark on a potentially groundbreaking initiative of negotiating drug prices directly with pharmaceutical manufacturers. This process, aimed at curbing the escalating costs of prescription drugs for Medicare beneficiaries, targets high-cost brand medications that have been on the market for a considerable length of time without generic or biosimilar competition.

The negotiation process is structured in phases. The initial round of negotiations began with the selection of ten drugs in 2023 (see Table 1), with negotiated *maximum fair prices* (MFPs) to take effect in 2026. Provided that the IRA remains intact under the Trump administration, future rounds in subsequent years will increase the number of "MFP" drugs to be included in negotiations. The process in each round will involve data submission from manufacturers, initial offers from CMS, and counter offers from the pharmaceutical companies, with the goal of reaching an agreement on MFP. If an agreement is not reached, the pharmaceutical company faces an excise tax on sales to Medicare beneficiaries.

CMS considers several factors in determining the MFP, including the clinical benefit of the drug, research and development costs, prices in other countries, and available alternatives. The objective of the Medicare negotiators in determining their MFP is to balance incentivizing pharmaceutical innovation with ensuring affordability for patients. Across the table, the ostensible objective of drug company negotiators is to make arguments that, for the sake of both

Table 1 Sales of ten companies of drugs subject to price negotiation under the Inflation Reduction Act of 2022, $ billions in FY2023

Company/ FY2023	MFP drug name	MFP drug sales, $b	Corporate US sales, $b	Corporate worldwide sales, $b
Amgen	Enbrel	3.7	19.3	26.9
Pfizer	Eliquis	4.2	26.7	57.2
Merck & Co.	Januvia	1.2	28.5	60.1
Eli Lilly	Jardiance	1.6	21.8	28.8
Bristol-Myers Squibb	Eliquis	8.6	31.5	43.8
Johnson & Johnson	Xarelto, Stelara, Imbruvica	10.4	31.2	54.8
AbbVie	Imbruvica	2.7	41.9	54.3
Novartis	Entresto	3.1	18.0	45.4
AstraZeneca	Farxiga	1.5	18.0	43.8
Novo Nordisk	Fiasp/NovoLog	0.8	18.5	33.7
Ten companies	**Ten MFP drugs**	37.6	255.4	448.8

Note: MFP drug = Maximum Fair Price drug (i.e., a drug subject to price negotiation with Medicare, as mandated by the Inflation Reduction Act).

Source: Company 10-K filings with the Securities and Exchange Commission

generating innovative drugs and making existing drugs more accessible, their company needs a price that is higher than that which CMS proposes.

Focusing on the first ten MFP drugs currently subject to price negotiation, the purpose of this Element is to equip government negotiators and regulators, as well as patient advocates, in the United States and elsewhere with a perspective on pharmaceutical drug pricing that seeks to create as much value as possible for society in the form of safe, effective, accessible, and affordable medicines. The implementation of this pricing task requires an understanding of how, through a social phenomenon that we call "collective and cumulative learning" (CCL), value is created in the pharmaceutical industry. CMS can then consider the impact of the MFP in incentivizing and enabling the pharmaceutical company to contribute to a value-creation process that results in safe, effective, accessible, and affordable medicines.

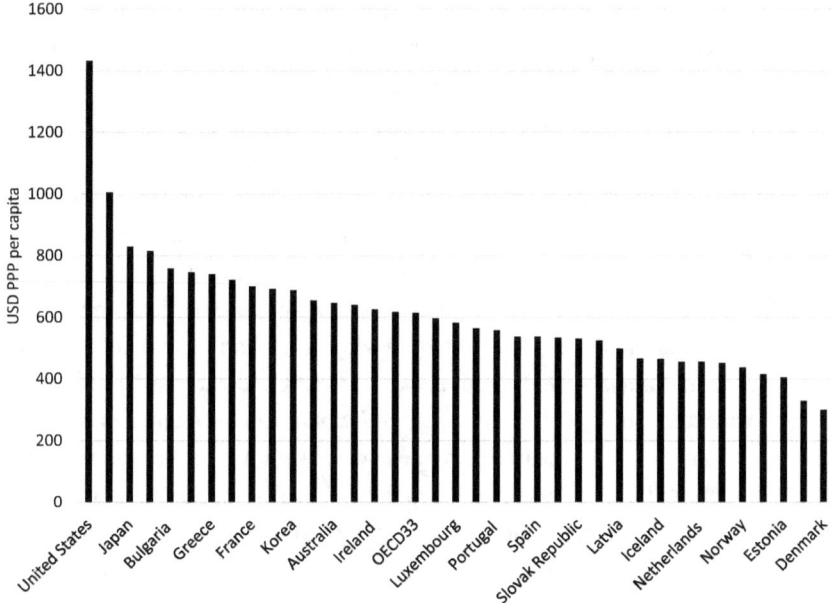

Figure 1 Expenditure on retail pharmaceuticals per capita, by OECD nation, 2021 (or nearest year)

Source: OECD (2023).

What is "collective and cumulative learning," and why is CCL so important (Lazonick 2019)? The innovation process that can generate a higher-quality, lower-cost product is uncertain, collective, and cumulative, and, hence, a theory of innovative enterprise must comprehend these characteristics of the innovation process.

- **Uncertain:** When investments in transforming technologies and accessing markets are made, the product and financial outcomes cannot be known in advance. If they were, the result would not be innovation. Hence the need for *strategy*.
- **Collective:** To generate a higher-quality, lower-cost product, the business enterprise must integrate the skills and efforts of large numbers of people with different hierarchical responsibilities and functional capabilities into the learning processes that are the essence of innovation. Hence the need for *organization*.
- **Cumulative:** Collective learning today enables collective learning tomorrow. These organizational-learning processes must be sustained continuously over time until financial returns can be generated through the sale of innovative products. Hence the need for *finance*.

Whether it be in business corporations, government agencies, civil-society organizations, or academic institutions, the research that is required for the development, manufacture, and delivery of an innovative drug requires CCL. The uncertain character of the innovation process means that when individuals supply their skills and efforts they cannot know whether their contributions will, in fact, result in a safe and effective drug. Typically, researchers are paid salaries to do their jobs with a view to creating value for society, but without the power to capture a portion of the value gained if and when an innovative drug is commercialized.

Our perspective on the relation between drug price and drug innovation focuses on investments in CCL not only within a pharmaceutical company that engages in *clinical research* but also antecedent and external to corporate-level pharmaceutical R&D to carry out *foundational research* and *translational research*. Foundational research provides society with a legacy of scientific advancements and technological developments, usually applicable to a range of industries besides pharmaceuticals, making it possible to engage in both translational research and clinical research, both of which are specific to the pharmaceutical industry. Translational research uses the knowledge and technologies of foundational research to focus on the phenotype or targeted drug discovery to address a specific disease. Clinical research is designed to develop a drug candidate that is sufficiently safe and effective to gain approval for commercial sale from the US Food and Drug Administration (FDA).

Clinical research, which generally occurs within the pharmaceutical company that is seeking to generate a commercial product, draws on the results of foundational and translational research as it seeks to develop a safe and effective drug. As a dynamic process, the results of clinical research can feed back to influence the direction of translational research, which can in turn provide insights that can make the knowledge and technologies that result from foundational research more relevant to the needs of the pharmaceutical industry. From this perspective, research performed by a pharmaceutical company is just one part of a lengthy and expansive CCL undertaken in and by "society" that can result in innovative drugs.

In negotiating an MFP, it is critical for CMS to understand the history of foundational, translational, and clinical research in the drug innovation process. For pharmaceutical companies, the price of a drug on the market performs two functions. It enables firms to cover the cost of the existing drug, while it also provides profits that can be reinvested by the company in the development of new drugs. CMS, however, should want to ensure that the MFP, by being set higher rather than lower, does not capture the value to society of drug innovation that has been created by foundational, translational, and, to some extent, clinical research that is antecedent and external to the pharmaceutical company with which they are negotiating. An MFP that is lower rather than higher permits drug users, that is, patients, rather than the pharmaceutical company, to capture a larger share of value to society.

In an era in which it is now taken for granted – in the United States at least – that the purpose of a business corporation is to "maximize shareholder value" (MSV), senior pharmaceutical executives tend to assume that, in selling the drug on the market, only their company is creating value to society in terms of costs avoided and benefits added from the alleviation of a disease. In drug-pricing discussions, the increasingly prevalent ideology emanating from the pharmaceutical industry is that the price that a company charges for a drug should reflect its value to society – a proposition known as "value-based pricing." But given the history of CCL in the foundational, translational, and clinical research that enables drug innovation, that position is at best misinformed and at worst self-serving.

In defense of value-based pricing, the firms can respond that the value to society of all that extra-firm research is embodied in the factor prices paid for physical and human inputs into the internal operations of the pharmaceutical company. There is a fundamental problem with this argument. In doing their work as participants in communities engaged in foundational, translational, and clinical research, scientists may be motivated by creating value for society. They are not, however, paid according to a "value-based pricing" model because the value of their work to society as measured by costs avoided and benefits added cannot be known until sometime in the highly uncertain, and often very distant, future when a safe and effective drug is put on the market.

People involved in scientific research and its technological applications expect to be paid "fairly," but the norms of "fairness" are far removed from the value that their work ultimately contributes to society. Indeed, even in a pharmaceutical company that seeks to impose value-based pricing, it will not necessarily be the employees of the firm that markets the drug who will capture the value-added of their work to society. MSV ideology contends that, in the drug development process, it is only shareholders, and not the company's employees, who make risky investment in drug innovation and who therefore have the sole claim to the company's profits, when they occur.

In arriving at their proposed MFP for a drug, CMS should take a stand against shareholder-driven value-based pricing on the grounds that a price that enables shareholders to lay claim to the value to society is bound to be grossly unfair. It will enable the company's shareholders, and indeed those best positioned among them, including the senior executives themselves, to capture value to society created by communities of scientists whose CCL has enabled foundational, translational, and clinical research.

In Section 2 of this Element, we explain why price regulation is needed in the pharmaceutical industry, notwithstanding warnings by pharmaceutical companies that any attempt to regulate drug prices will come at the cost of innovation. The companies contend that high prices on drugs already approved by the Food and Drug Administration (FDA) and for sale on the market will provide them with the revenues and profits they need to invest in the next round of drug innovation. In principle, we concur with this argument, but it leaves open the critical question of how high those drug prices need to be to perform this financing function.

For the case of the United States, we document that the pharmaceutical companies whose drug prices are being negotiated spend all their profits, and often more, on distributions to shareholders. They do not use profits from existing drugs on the market to fund investment in the next generation of innovative medicines. Pharmaceutical executives contend that these distributions to shareholders are necessary to induce them to fund drug innovation. We show that the public shareholders to whom they are funneling corporate cash do not fund investment in productive capabilities; they simply buy and sell shares outstanding on the market. The same corporate executives who make these flawed arguments benefit personally from distributions to shareholders through their copious stock-based pay. Indeed, in some cases it appears that drug companies even take on debt to pursue their foremost resource-allocation priority: dividends and buybacks for the sake of "maximizing shareholder value."

Legitimizing this behavior is the fallacious MSV ideology, dominant in US corporate governance, that *only* shareholders take risk in investing in the productive capabilities that are essential for innovation. We argue that households as workers and as taxpayers invest in innovation, and hence have a claim on profits when they occur. Comparatively, shareholders of a publicly listed corporation take little risk because, by selling their shares on the liquid stock market, they can convert their share portfolios to cash at low cost at any point in time.

We conclude Section 2 on what is a fair drug price, with critical analyses of the statements of two prominent pharmaceutical CEOs – Kenneth Frazier of Merck (2011–2021) and Albert Bourla of Pfizer (2019 to the present) – on the appropriateness of "value-based pricing" of the drugs that their companies sell. As already indicated, there are two fundamental problems with this argument. The first problem is that, given the dominance of MSV as a theory of value creation, value-based pricing rewards those participants in the corporation who make the least contributions to value creation. The second problem is that the value captured in a high drug price includes value created by foundational, translational, and, to some extent, clinical research which, through CCL by the relevant scientific communities, generates knowledge and technologies that enable investments in CCL by the pharmaceutical company seeking to develop, manufacture, and deliver a safe, effective, accessible, and affordable drug.

After having exposed the first problem in Section 2, we turn in Section 3 to explaining the second problem by providing a perspective on the linkages among foundational, translational, and clinical research that enable pharmaceutical companies to engage in CCL for drug innovation. Then in Section 4, we focus in empirical detail on the translational research that enabled the development of the ten MFP drugs, the prices of which are currently under negotiation. In Section 5, we summarize the implications of our arguments and findings for government negotiators as they try to arrive at a "maximum fair price."

2 What Is a "Fair" Drug Price?
Rising Drug Costs under Medicare Part D

For decades, the US pharmaceutical industry has played a vital role in discovering and developing safe and effective medicines, notwithstanding some major missteps such as Merck's Vioxx and Purdue's Oxycontin along the way (Prakash and Valentine 2007). Even when new prescription drugs are safe and effective, however, they have not necessarily been accessible and affordable (Collington and Lazonick 2022). Some of the blame for high drug costs can be laid at the door of the US system of health insurance, which defies the logic of economic efficiency by, uniquely among the rich nations, eschewing a single-payer insurance provider. Or one might point to the opaque, inefficient, and possibly corrupt influence of pharmaceutical benefits managers (PBMs), who negotiate drug prices with pharmaceutical companies, health insurers, and pharmacies, leaving US households and taxpayers to foot the expensive prescription bills. Nevertheless, the pharmaceutical companies have participated in making the drugs they sell less accessible and affordable than they could be, even though the US government plays a major role in funding the foundational and translational research that pharmaceutical companies need to engage in clinical research, and then grants these companies patent monopolies and market exclusivity that empower them to set high drug prices.

The problems of inaccessible and unaffordable medicines in the United States are not new. During a 1983 hearing on a proposed bill to restore the patent life of prescription drugs, critics such as Senator Howard Metzenbaum and consumer advocate Ralph Nader accused pharmaceutical companies of exploiting their monopolies on patented drugs by charging exorbitant prices that made essential medications unaffordable to many Americans (U.S. Congress 1983). During a 1985 House hearing on prescription drug price increases in the United States, Representative Henry Waxman, who, until he retired in 2015 after forty years in Congress, was a key critic of high drug prices, voiced his concern: "The prices we pay for brand name drugs in this country are just outrageous. The drug industry is making obscene profits, and the American people are paying the price" (Horwitz 1985).

Reformers proposed that, once patents expired, competition from generic drugs could halt escalating drug prices. Bipartisan support in Congress for legislation to balance the interests of brand and generic drug manufacturers ultimately resulted in passage of the Drug Price Competition and Patent Term Restoration Act of 1984, also known as the Hatch-Waxman Act. This legislation aimed to streamline the approval process for generic drugs while providing incentives for innovation.

In seeking to strike a balance between promoting generic competition and providing incentives for pharmaceutical companies to invest in drug R&D, the Hatch-Waxman Act extends the patent monopoly period for brand drugs to compensate for patent-life time lost during the clinical trials and the regulatory approval process. Under its "data exclusivity" provision, the Act also provides a brand drug approved under "new chemical entity" designation with five-year market protection against generic competition, regardless of the drug's patent status. Furthermore, the Act grants an additional three-year exclusivity for previously approved drugs under the "new clinical investigation" provision when there is (a) a change in the drug's formulation, dosage, administration, schedule, and so on; (b) demonstrated efficacy in any new indication (e.g., a drug previously approved for breast cancer shows efficacy for prostate cancer); or (c) confirmation of its safety in a new patient population (e.g., people in certain age groups or people with certain existing and/or pre-existing health conditions) (U.S. Congress 1984).

The US Orphan Drug Act (ODA) of 1983 provides financial subsidies and market protection for pharmaceutical companies to develop drugs for rare and genetic diseases (Lazonick and Tulum 2011). From January 1, 1983, through December 31, 2024, there were 7,210 ODA designations and 1,295 ODA approvals (FDA 2024). ODA also offers R&D tax credits and FDA assistance in ensuring the rapid transformation of a promising compound into an approved marketable drug. Of great importance, ODA approvals provide seven-year marketing exclusivity for a specific indication from the date that it receives FDA approval for commercial use.

These provisions permit pharmaceutical companies to maintain market exclusivity for their innovative products for a longer duration, enabling a greater return on R&D investments that culminated in approved products. As an additional gift to pharmaceutical companies in extending their monopoly power, in 1995 the duration of patent protection was increased to twenty years from the seventeen years that had prevailed from 1861 through 1994 (USPTO 2024). With technological change, one patented drug can be replaced with a superior patented drug, and, although the fortunes of different pharmaceutical companies may change, the "solution" of generic competition for certain indications may never see the opportunity to lower prices.

In the context of this permissive legislative environment, prescription drug price rises have increasingly surpassed general price inflation from the early 1980s to the present. Figure 2 graphs the changes in the average prices of consumer prescription drugs (CPI-Rx: Triangle line), medical care (CPI-MC: Dashed line), and all consumer products (CPI-All: Solid line) for 1982 to 2023 Q2. In the top figure (a), the base index years for the changes observed for the three groups are 1982–1984, the years that led to the passage of the Hatch-Waxman Act. The index base years for the graphs in the bottom-left (b) and bottom-right (c) are, respectively, 2003, the passage of the Medicare Modernization Act (MMA) establishing the Medicare Part D Program (also known as Medicare Prescription Drug Plan or PDP), and 2010, the passage of the Affordable Care Act (ACA).

Figure 2(a) shows a limited impact on pharmaceutical prices of generic drug entry into the market following the enactment of the Hatch-Waxman Act in 1984, as the growth in CPI-Rx significantly exceeded CPI-All between 1983 and the second quarter of 2023. In Figure 2(b), with prices indexed to 2003, the gap between CPI-Rx and CPI-All gradually widened in the decade after PDP went into effect in 2006, with Medicare now covering prescription drug expenses for over three million eligible enrollees. Figure 2(c), with prices indexed to 2010, demonstrates that CPI-Rx growth outpaced CPI-MC during the five-year period after major provisions of the ACA took effect in 2014. Following the introduction of President Biden's "Build Back Better" plan in 2021, however, for the first time since the introduction of the Hatch-Waxman Act in 1984, CPI-Rx growth began to slow compared to both the CPI-MC and CPI-All indices.

Medicare Part D Program prior to the IRA

Medicare PDP, introduced in 2003 through the MMA, aims to address a significant gap in healthcare coverage for older adults: the lack of comprehensive prescription drug benefits. Prior to PDP, many seniors were often forced to ration or forgo necessary medications due to high out-of-pocket costs. The MMA sought to alleviate these problems by creating a voluntary outpatient

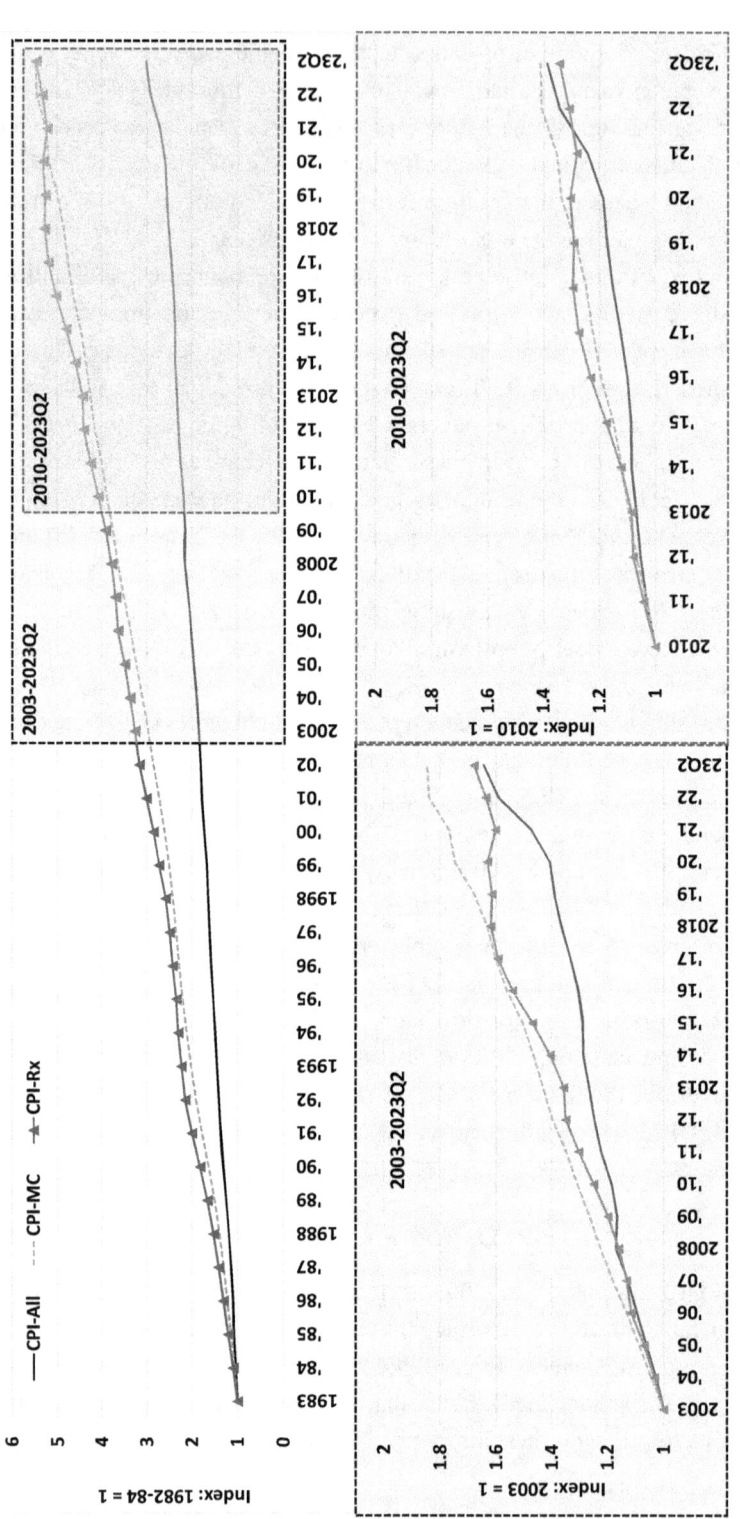

Figure 2 Changes in consumer price index for medical care (CPI-MC), prescription drugs (CPI-Rx), all consumer products (CPI-All)

Sources: BLS (2023), All Items in U.S. City Average, All Urban Consumers, Not Seasonally Adjusted (CPI-All, CUUR0000SA0); Medical Care in U.S. City Average, All Urban Consumers, Seasonally Adjusted (CPI-MC, CUUR0000SAM); Prescription Drugs in U.S. City Average, All Urban Consumers, Not Seasonally Adjusted (CPI-Rx, CUUR0000SEMF01.

prescription drug benefit offered through private plans, with subsidies available to low-income beneficiaries.

The establishment of PDP sparked intense debate and controversy, particularly regarding the prohibition of direct price negotiation between Medicare and drug manufacturers. This restriction, a result of heavy lobbying by the pharmaceutical industry, prevented Medicare from leveraging its purchasing power to secure lower drug prices for beneficiaries (Stolberg and Robbins 2023). Critics argued that this provision favored the industry's profits over patient affordability, contributing to escalating drug costs. An analysis published in the *Journal of the American Medical Association* (*JAMA*) in 2017 estimated that Medicare could have saved billions of dollars if it had been allowed to negotiate drug prices directly (Venker et al. 2019).

A contentious issue that arose from the exclusion of the regulatory power to negotiate directly with manufacturers to control drug prices was the emergence of the "donut hole," a coverage gap in the standard Part D benefit. This gap occurred when a beneficiary's total drug spending exceeded a certain threshold, leaving them responsible for a significant portion of the costs until reaching the catastrophic coverage level. In 2012, a study highlighted declining adherence to antihypertensive and lipid-lowering medications among the PDP enrollees due to increased out-of-pocket spending caused by the growing coverage gap (Roumie 2012).

In 2010, ACA sought to address the donut hole by gradually reducing the beneficiary's share of costs during this gap. ACA introduced discounts from drug manufacturers and government subsidies to eliminate the coverage gap. Eventually, these provisions, coupled with subsequent modifications, significantly lowered out-of-pocket costs for beneficiaries and improved access to medications (Span 2020).

ACA brought about major transformations in the healthcare landscape, particularly through the Biologics Price Competition and Innovation Act and the Health Care and Education Reconciliation Act. These legislative measures impacted the regulatory framework governing biosimilars, insurance plans, and Medicare Part D. Consequently, a reevaluation of reimbursement policies and payment systems became imperative within the biopharmaceutical products market.

Amid ongoing political uncertainty surrounding ACA's future, large pharmaceutical companies shifted their focus from mass markets and blockbuster drugs toward more specialized markets. A prime example of this shift was Hoffman-La Roche's development of a product portfolio centered on specialty drugs, which face less competitive price pressure (Tulum 2018). Other major biopharmaceutical companies also targeted niche segments of the drug market with products offering higher profit margins as a means of mitigating price pressures. Orphan drugs, which receive priority reviews and regulatory assistance from the FDA, emerged as an area of heightened interest due to their exemption from market competition for seven years after FDA approval (Lazonick and Tulum 2011).

Pharmaceutical companies also faced revenue declines as patents for blockbuster drugs expired, paving the way for generic drug makers to enter the market with lower-priced alternatives. In response, these companies explored new marketing strategies, such as expanding into premium product markets and acquiring major generic drug makers. To safeguard their market shares against generic drugs, brand drug companies often resorted to filing legal claims to delay the entry of generic producers into the market. Another tactic that they employed was a confidential arrangement known as a "reverse payment" patent settlement or "pay-for-delay" agreement, which essentially compensated generic drug manufacturers for delaying the launch of their generic versions of brand drugs (Feldman 2022). Notably, efforts to pass legislation specifically prohibiting reverse payments, such as the Preserve Access to Affordable Generics Act, have been unsuccessful since their introduction in 2007.

The Inflation Reduction Act of 2022 seeks to mitigate persistently rising drug prices. The IRA was not a stand-alone bill; it emerged as a slimmed-down version of President Biden's earlier Build Back Better agenda, which is a government investment plan encompassing a wide range of social spending and climate initiatives. The bill faced significant opposition due to its high price tag and certain tax-the-rich provisions. To secure its passage, the Biden administration drastically scaled it back and refocused it on key priorities like climate change, healthcare costs, and deficit reduction. This revised version, the Inflation Reduction Act (IRA), ultimately garnered the necessary support for passage and was signed into law in August 2022.

The IRA marked a significant turning point in government intervention in the pharmaceutical industry by finally allowing Medicare to directly negotiate prices for a select group of high-cost drugs. This landmark change was met with fierce opposition from the pharmaceutical companies and their trade association Pharmaceutical Research and Manufacturers of America (PhRMA), but proponents argued that it was essential for curbing excessive drug spending and ensuring affordability for Medicare beneficiaries. According to a Congressional Budget Office report, the IRA's drug pricing provisions are projected to save Medicare nearly $100 billion over the next decade (CBO 2023). The IRA also includes provisions to cap out-of-pocket costs for insulin under Part D and eliminate cost-sharing for adult vaccines covered by the program. The purpose of these measures is to enhance access of seniors to essential medications and preventive care.

Medicare PDP has undergone significant evolution since its inception in 2003. While initially facing criticism for its lack of price negotiation authority and the burden of the donut hole, subsequent legislation like the ACA and IRA have made substantial progress in addressing these issues. The debate over drug pricing and access remains ongoing, but the recent reforms represent a potentially significant step toward ensuring that Medicare beneficiaries can afford the medications they need to maintain their health and well-being. Improved access to medications can lead to better management of chronic conditions, reduced hospitalization rates, and enhanced overall health.

None of these outcomes is assured, however. It depends on how the CMS negotiates prices. It depends on what they accept as a "maximum fair price."

Characteristics of the Ten MFP Drugs

To ensure that the drug-price negotiation process targets medications with the greatest impact on affordability, the IRA has established stringent criteria for selection as an MFP drug. The drug must be covered under Medicare Part D, the program specifically designed for prescription drug benefits, so that the negotiations directly address the medications most relevant to Medicare recipients. Only brand drugs without generic or biosimilar alternatives are eligible for negotiation, as these tend to be the most expensive and lack competition that could drive prices down. Additionally, the IRA prioritizes drugs that are among the most expensive covered by Medicare and are used by significant numbers of beneficiaries. This approach targets medications that have the largest financial impact on both the program and patients.

The initial list of ten drugs was published on September 1, 2023, with negotiations beginning the following month and ending on August 1, 2024. The MFPs negotiated for the ten drugs were announced on August 15, 2024 (The White House 2024). CMS is expected to sign agreements with the manufacturers by March 1, 2025, for the finalized MFP that will take effect in January 2026. Crucially, in ensuring a continuous effort to tackle high drug prices, the IRA mandates annual negotiations for at least fifteen additional drugs each year thereafter, with the second round starting in January 2027 for the new negotiated prices to take effect in 2028.

The drugs which CMS selected for negotiation include some of the leading prescription drugs in the United States, with classes of therapies that include (a) anticoagulant, medications that prevent blood clotting; (b) antidiabetic and cardiovascular, (c) antirheumatic; and (d) anticancer drugs (see Table 2). The diseases treated by these drugs are among the leading causes of morbidity and mortality in the United States, resulting in disability or premature death, and

Table 2 Total PDP gross covered prescription drug costs and numbers of drug users, June 2022–May 2023

Therapy class	Drug (approved indication)	Period cost, $b	Number of users, 000s
Anticoagulants	Eliquis (blood clots)	16.5	3,706
	Xarelto (blood clots)	6.0	1,337
Antidiabetics and cardiovascular drugs	Fiasp/NovoLog (diabetes)	2.6	777
	Januvia (diabetes)	4.1	869
	Farxiga (diabetes, heart failure)	3.3	799
	Jardiance (diabetes, heart failure)	7.1	1,573
	Entresto (heart failure)	2.9	587
Disease-modifying antirheumatics	Enbrel (RA; psoriasis; PA)	2.8	48
	Stelara (psoriasis; PA)	2.6	22
Anticancer	Imbruvica (cancer)	2.7	20

Notes: PA = psoriatic arthritis; RA = rheumatoid arthritis.
Sources: CMS (2023).

imposing an immense economic burden upon individuals, families, and society as a whole.

In 2022, heart disease, the leading cause of death in the United States, claimed the lives of over 700,000 people (CDC 2023a). It is a major public health concern, affecting millions of Americans and significantly contributing to healthcare expenditures and lost productivity. Cancer, the second leading cause of death, was responsible for over 600,000 deaths in 2023 (Siegel et al. 2023). It encompasses a wide range of diseases, each with its own unique characteristics and treatment challenges. Diabetes, affecting over thirty-eight million Americans, was the eighth leading cause of death in 2021 (CDC 2023b). It is a chronic disease that can lead to serious complications, including heart disease, stroke, kidney failure, and blindness. Affecting nearly one million Americans, blood clotting claims up to 100,000 deaths each year, and is the fifth common cause of unplanned rehospitalization following a surgery that leads to serious complications such as stroke, heart attack, and deep vein thrombosis (CDC 2024). Rheumatoid arthritis, a chronic autoimmune disease that affects over 1.5 million Americans (Arthritis Foundation 2024), causes joint pain, swelling, and stiffness, leading to functional limitations and reduced quality of life. These diseases have a devastating impact on individuals and families while placing a significant burden on the healthcare system and the economy.

The US government is a large, and generous, purchaser of pharmaceutical products in the United States. From June 2022 to May 2023, the US government spent $50.5 billion on the ten MFP drugs for 8.3 million Medicare Part D program (PDP) enrollees, accounting for 20 percent of the total PDP spending on prescription drugs. The total gross covered[1] prescription drug costs of anticoagulant drugs Eliquis and Xarelto, which over five million PDP patients used for the treatment of blood clots, was $22.5 billion (Table 2). With an average cost of $4,500 per enrollee, these two products alone accounted for 45 percent of the total $50.5 billion spent on all ten drugs subject to price negotiations

Three Conceptual Preparatory Steps to Negotiate a Maximum Fair Price

The implementation of these negotiations will undoubtedly face ongoing debate and legal challenges. The pharmaceutical industry has voiced concerns about the potential impact on innovation, while patient advocates and policymakers underscore the critical need for affordable medicines. The future of drug pricing in the United States will depend on the outcomes of these negotiations, with important implications for evolving political positions and debates on healthcare policy.

Presumably, the purpose of price regulation is to support the generation of safe, effective, accessible, and affordable medicines. The government's major weakness in drug-price negotiations is Medicare's lack of a framework for identifying how a "fair" price can contribute to the achievement of this purpose. The first step in defining a "fair" price is to explain why there is a need for government regulation of drug prices. The second step is to articulate how, in theory, a drug price on an existing product can support new investment in safe, effective, accessible, and affordable medicines. The third step is to determine whether in practice a negotiated drug price would incentivize and empower corporate behavior that would significantly improve the availability of safe, effective, accessible, and affordable medicines.

Step One: More than perhaps any other industry, drug development, manufacturing, and delivery requires corporate investments in collective and cumulative learning (CCL), which, along with investments in plant and equipment, represent a fixed cost; that is, a cost that the firm must incur regardless of how much output is produced. Subsequent to FDA approval of a drug as safe and effective for use, the pharmaceutical company that controls the marketing of the

---

[1] Gross covered prescription drug costs are actually paid costs incurred under PDP during the coverage year, which includes all fees related to the dispensing of medications except for the administrative costs.

drug seeks to transform the high fixed cost incurred in developing the drug into a low unit cost by reaping economies of scale through the delivery of the drug to large numbers of patients. The firm incurs additions to fixed cost in making the drug accessible to patients through investments in facilities and personnel for mass production (including the cost of maintaining quality as the firm scales production) and mass distribution (including, in the United States, advertising the drug). Given the firm's fixed cost of developing, manufacturing, and delivering the drug, the greater the number of patients to whom the firm sells the product, the lower the unit cost of the product, and hence the more *potentially* affordable the drug. The *actual* affordability to the government and patients depends on how the drug is priced.

This transformation of high fixed cost into low unit cost is represented in the cost curve in Figure 3.[2] Given publicly funded government investment in knowledge embodied in drug development, the firm's cost structure does not usually come close to fully accounting for the social cost of bringing a drug to market. Moreover, the unit cost of a drug is only meaningful when output is delivered to patients. Given the uncertainty of the innovation process, a drug candidate in which the firm invests may fail to yield a safe and effective product that can be submitted for FDA approval, in which case the firm can incur substantial fixed cost without its transformation into low unit cost.

There is a need for drug-price regulation because with economies of scale, reflected in a downward sloping cost curve in Figure 3, there can be no equilibrium of supply and demand to set a market price, as in textbook theories of the firm (Lazonick 2023a; Lazonick 2024, pp. 58–89). Given that a pharmaceutical drug is a necessity – often a matter of life or death – for diseased patients, the demand curve, which determines revenues from the sale of the drug at a given price, exhibits low or no price elasticity of demand (as shown in Figure 3). Without drug-price regulation, the pharmaceutical company can charge higher prices without the reduction in demand that would occur in the presence of a price-elastic (downward-sloping) demand curve. The higher the price charged for a given level of demand for the drug, the higher the profits of the pharmaceutical company that is selling the drug.

Step Two: Now that we have explained why drug-price regulation is needed, we can articulate how, in theory, a drug price on an existing product can support the generation of safe, effective, accessible, and affordable medicines. For a given level of sold output per year, the product's price determines the amount of revenues that the firm has available to allocate for the next year to distribute

---

[2] The following discussion draws on Collington and Lazonick (2022). For an elaboration of the theory of innovative enterprise, see Lazonick (2019).

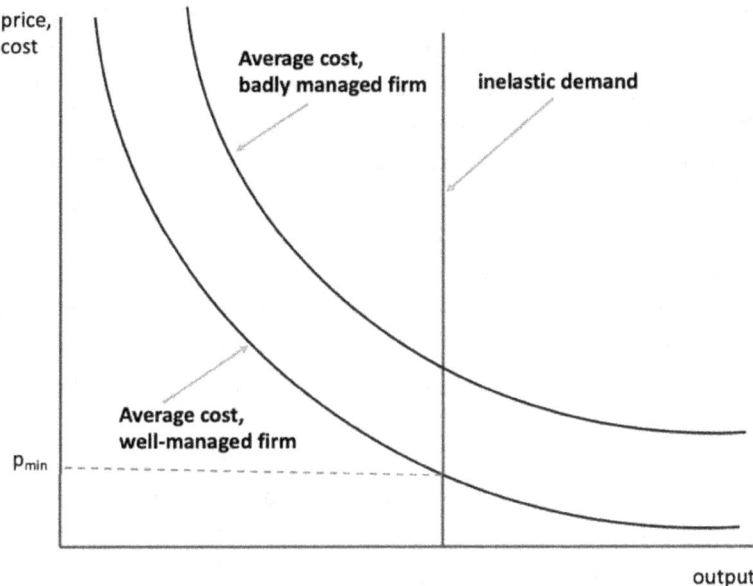

Figure 3 The innovating firm's cost and revenue curves for a pharmaceutical drug

to its stakeholders, most notably employees and shareholders, and reinvest in the business. If the firm makes a profit (revenues greater than costs) for the year, senior management has surplus funds available for stakeholder distributions and/or corporate reinvestment.

In arguing for a specific MFP, the CMS could seek a price that is so low that it leaves no profits available to the firm, but which makes the drug as affordable as possible to patients. Alternatively, the CMS could agree to negotiate a higher price that provides the pharmaceutical company with profits that it can reinvest in new drug development, sacrificing affordability on the existing MFP drug. In practice, in setting an MFP, the CMS is choosing a tradeoff between increased affordability of the existing drug and corporate reinvestment in new drug development.

For their part, the pharmaceutical company could push for an MFP that provides high profits, contending that it requires these funds to finance investment in new drug development. In fact, for decades, when faced with complaints about high drug prices, the US pharmaceutical industry has responded that lower drug prices that would make existing drugs more affordable would mean a reduction in the amount of funds that pharmaceutical companies would be able to allocate to drug innovation.

For example, when, in 1985, the *Washington Post* reported that Representative Henry Waxman had accused pharmaceutical companies of "outrageous price increases" and "greed on a massive scale," pharmaceutical executives responded that "prices have climbed recently to cover accelerated investment in researching and developing new and better medications to protect Americans" (Horwitz 1985). More recently, drug executives have complained that, even with unregulated prices, the rise of PBMs as powerful actors in the price-setting process has deprived the drug companies of profits needed for investment in innovation (PhRMA 2024a). In 2022, in opposition to the passage of the IRA, PhRMA argued that the IRA's pricing proposal "makes a broken system worse by disincentivizing the research and development needed to find new treatments and cures" (Longo 2022).

On August 4, 2022 – on the eve of the IRA being signed into law – PhRMA president Stephen Ubl and thirty-one senior pharmaceutical executives (mostly CEOs) who sit on PhRMA's board of directors wrote a letter in which they sounded the alarm on drug-price regulation under the IRA:

> While the bill saves the federal government $300 billion, it takes far more from the biopharmaceutical industry and will have significant consequences for innovation and patients' hope for the future. Some economists estimate upwards of 100 new treatments may be sacrificed over the next two decades if this bill becomes law. This includes treatments for multiple chronic conditions, the annual $2.7 trillion medical and lost productivity costs of which far exceed the direct federal "savings" this bill would achieve. (Ubl 2022)

Subsequently, on June 6, 2023, with price negotiations under the IRA ramping up, US-based Merck announced that it had filed a complaint against the US Department of Health and Human Services, contesting its right to mandate negotiation of drug prices. In a letter to the "Merck community," the company wrote: "By changing the incentives and returns for some therapies and technologies over others, the IRA is changing the course of R&D, which in time will leave many patients without treatment options" (Davis et al. 2022).

Step Three: In making these statements about the possible implications of drug-price regulation on the financing of drug innovation, pharmaceutical executives and their representatives are making a *potentially* valid point. There is overwhelming evidence from industry studies, including pharmaceuticals, that, for an established company with profitable products on the market, retained profits are the foundation of committed finance to fund the growth of the firm, including new product innovation. The question that needs to be asked, however, is whether pharmaceutical companies that are selling drugs in the US market at high, unregulated prices are in fact using those profits to finance drug innovation.

The clear-cut answer to this question is that they are not. Table 3 documents the extent to which major US-based pharmaceutical corporations have been allocating their net income to distributions to shareholders in the form of cash dividends and stock buybacks. Of the 478 corporations in the S&P 500 Index in September 2023 that were publicly traded from 2013 through 2022, 14 are pharmaceutical companies. In the aggregate, these 478 corporations distributed $6.4 trillion as stock buybacks during their 2013–2022 fiscal years, representing 57 percent of net income, and $4.5 trillion as cash dividends, an additional 40 percent of net income (see Table 3). We estimate that 95 percent of these stock buybacks were done as open-market repurchases (OMRs) of common shares, the main purpose of which is to manipulate the company's stock price.

As shown in Table 3, for the decade 2013–2022, the 14 pharmaceutical companies among the 478 companies in the dataset distributed 105 percent of net income to shareholders, a larger proportion than the highly financialized 98 percent for all 478 companies.[3] These 14 pharmaceutical companies accounted for 3.2 percent of the revenues of all 478 companies but 6.6 percent of the net income, 5.8 percent of the buybacks, and 8.9 percent of the dividends. At 51 percent, pharmaceutical stock buybacks were below the proportion of 57 percent of net income for the 478 companies, but, at 54 percent versus 40 percent, pharmaceutical dividends as a proportion of net income far exceeded that of all the companies in the dataset.

The $773 billion that the pharmaceutical companies distributed to shareholders was 10 percent greater than the $701 billion that these corporations expended on R&D over the decade.

Of the top eight pharmaceutical corporations in terms of distributions to shareholders as a percent of net income in Table 3, seven companies, excluding Baxter, are the manufacturers of drugs that CMS has selected for the first round of IRA price negotiations (see Table 1, in which the companies with which CMS is negotiating are in boldface): Eliquis for blood clots (BMS and Pfizer); Imbruvica for cancer (AbbVie and J&J); Enbrel for psoriatic and rheumatoid arthritis (Amgen and Pfizer); Januvia for diabetes (Merck); Stelara for psoriatic arthritis and Xarelto for blood clots (J&J); and Jardiance for diabetes and heart failure (Eli Lilly). During 2013–2022, the Medicare Part D program spent $173 billion on these drugs, accounting for over seven percent of the net sales of pharmaceutical products ($2.6 trillion) reported by these seven companies.

The other three companies – Novartis (Entresto), and Novo Nordisk (Fiasp/ NovoLog), and AstraZeneca (Farxiga) – are non-US-based companies. In

---

[3] Note that, in an accounting period (e.g., a decade), a company can distribute more than 100 percent of profits to shareholders by taking on debt, laying off workers, divesting assets, and/or using cash reserves (including those that represent capital consumption allowances).

Table 3 Financial data, 2013–2022, and 2022 employment, for 478 corporations, of which 14 are pharmaceutical companies, in the S&P 500 Index publicly listed for fiscal years 2013–2022

Company (year founded; IPO)	2013–2022 Totals, $b						% of NI			R&D, % of REV	2022 EMP. (000s)
	REV	NI	BB	DV	DV+BB	R&D	BB	DV	BB+DV		
BMS (1858; 1928)	273	24	27	31	57	82	110	127	236	30	34
AbbVie (1888; 1929)	342	64	32	55	87	62	50	87	137	18	50
Amgen (1980; 1983)	231	63	50	31	81	43	79	49	129	19	25
Merck (1891; 1941)	451	78	42	57	98	99	54	73	127	22	69
J&J (1886; 1944)	799	147	57	93	150	114	38	63	102	14	156
Eli Lilly (1870; 1952)	235	42	16	25	41	63	38	59	98	27	39
Baxter (1931; 1978)	125	14	7	6	13	7	52	44	96	6	60
Pfizer (1849; 1941)	584	157	61	77	138	93	39	49	88	16	83
Biogen (1978; 1983)	114	34	28	0	28	24	84	0	84	21	9
Gilead Sciences (1987; 1992)	249	73	36	24	60	56	49	33	82	22	17
Viatris (1971; 1978)	116	4	2	1	3	7	53	24	77	6	37
Regeneron (1988; 1991)	71	24	13	0	13	23	53	0	53	32	12
Vertex (1989; 1999)	37	10	3	0	3	16	30	0	30	43	5
Incyte (1991; 1993)	17	1	0	0	0	11	5	0	5	61	2
Total 14 Pharma	**3,643**	**734**	**373**	**400**	**773**	**701**	**51**	**54**	**105**	**19**	**598**

	REV	NI	BB	DV	R&D	IPO	EE
Total 478 in S&P500	1,15,333	11,103	6,368	4,491	10,860	3,269	57	40	98	3	28,329
14 Pharma as % of 478 in S&P 500 = 2.9%	3.20%	6.60%	5.80%	8.90%	7.10%	21.40%					2.10%
AstraZeneca (1999; 1999)	277	23	0	36	36	62	0	157	157	22	84
Novartis (1996; 1996)	508	110	47	68	115	93	43	62	105	18	102
Novo Nordisk (1923; 1974)	183	60	21	19	40	24	35	32	67	13	55

Notes: IPO = initial public offering, REV = revenues, NI = net income, BB = stock buybacks, DV = dividends, R&D = research & development expenditures, EE = end-of-fiscal-year employment (in thousands); J&J is Johnson & Johnson; BMS is Bristol Myers Squibb; Baxter is Baxter International. The founding and IPO years listed for AbbVie are those of its predecessor company Abbott Laboratories; for BMS, the founding of Squibb and the IPO of Bristol-Myers; and for Viatris, its predecessor company Mylan.

Sources: S&P Compustat database and company 10-K and 20-F reports.

2013–2022, Novartis had $110 billion in net income, of which $68 billion were distributed as dividends (62 percent) and $47 billion as buybacks (42 percent). Over the decade, the company spent 23 percent more on distributions to shareholders than on R&D, with R&D/sales at 18 percent.

In 2013–2022, Novo Nordisk had $60 billion in net income, of which $27 billion were distributed as dividends (45 percent) and $26 billion as buybacks (44 percent). It should be noted that about 30 percent of the dividends and 18 percent of the buybacks were distributions to Novo Holding A/S, an industrial foundation that has voting control over Novo Nordisk. Over the decade, Novo Nordisk spent 41 percent more on distributions to shareholders than on R&D, with R&D/sales at 13 percent.

Alone among the ten companies with which Medicare is negotiating drug prices, AstraZeneca did no buybacks during 2013–2022. After more than a decade of financialized behavior beginning with the merger that created the company in 1999, AstraZeneca's board made the conscious decision to cease buybacks as of 2013 for the sake of investing in its drug pipeline (Tulum et al. 2023). The $62 billion spent on R&D over the decade were 23 percent of sales. Nevertheless, at the same time, the company paid out $36 billion in dividends, equal to 157 percent of net income.

Prime beneficiaries of distributions to shareholders have been the very same senior executives who control the pharmaceutical companies' resource-allocation decisions. Table 4 displays data on the compensation of the 500 highest-paid executives in the United States for each year from 2006 through 2022 and the subset of pharmaceutical executives among these 500 highest paid.

From 2006 through 2022, the average total direct compensation (TDC) of the 500 highest-paid executives ranged from, with the stock market depressed, a low of $15.9 million in 2009, of which 60 percent were realized gains from stock-based pay, to, with the stock market booming, a high of $49.1 million in 2021, of which 89 percent were realized gains from stock-based pay. In 2022, the average TDC of 500 highest-paid executives in 2022 was $35.9 million, of which 85 percent were realized gains from stock-based pay. In 2021, when the average TDC of the two comparison groups peaked, pharmaceutical executives' average TDC of $66.9 million was significantly higher than for the 500 highest-paid executives.[4]

Not even the SEC, which purportedly regulates US financial markets, knows the precise days on which buybacks as OMRs are executed. But the CEO and

---

[4] Note that these data include realized gains from executives' stock-based compensation, the correct measure of the take-home pay of these executives, on which they pay taxes to the US Treasury. Almost all data on stock-based compensation reported by the media, and even most progressive think tanks, are grant-date (so-called "fair value") measures, which ignore the stock-price increases that actually inflate executive pay – and hence the ways in which this pay is

Table 4 500 highest-paid executives annually, US corporations and subset of pharmaceutical executives, with proportions of mean total direct compensation (TDC) from stock options and stock awards, 2006–2022

	All 500 highest-paid executives				Pharma executives				
	Mean, $m	% of TDC			Mean, $m	% of TDC			
Year	TDC	SO	SA	SO+SA	TDC	SO	SA	SO+SA	No. of execs
2006	25.6	56	17	73	25.7	47	30	77	23
2007	31.5	57	19	76	22.1	65	8	73	14
2008	20.7	48	23	71	22.1	64	13	76	21
2009	15.9	37	23	60	22.0	40	18	59	29
2010	19.8	38	26	65	20.8	50	24	74	25
2011	21.7	39	30	69	20.6	55	15	71	24
2012	32.3	41	37	78	34.9	61	24	85	24
2013	27.4	46	33	79	35.3	68	24	91	34
2014	32.7	46	34	80	43.7	69	19	88	41
2015	35.0	49	35	84	46.2	58	30	88	32
2016	27.5	37	42	78	31.5	48	23	71	26
2017	33.8	46	35	82	43.5	52	37	89	22
2018	33.6	43	42	85	34.5	67	21	88	22
2019	33.6	40	43	82	38.2	60	26	86	19
2020	43.4	52	35	87	49.7	63	27	90	31
2021	49.1	45	43	89	66.9	83	11	94	24
2022	35.9	30	55	85	45.0	64	24	88	28

Note: TDC = total direct compensation, SO = stock options, SA = stock awards
Source: S&P ExecuComp database

CFO of the corporation doing the buybacks possess this material insider information, and, moreover, they exercise control over when buybacks are done. Under any circumstances, other things equal, OMRs will result in stock-price increases that augment the stock-based pay of senior executives, while strategic control over and insider information about the timing of these buybacks can further contribute to the gains that senior corporate executives realize in exercising stock options and the vesting of stock awards.

---

inflated. See Hopkins and Lazonick (2016); Lazonick and Hopkins (2016); Lazonick and Hopkins (2017). See also Hopkins and Lazonick (2024).

Distributions to Shareholders at Merck and Pfizer

Tables 5 and 6 show distributions to shareholders, 1978–2022, by Merck and Pfizer, two Big Pharma companies that for decades have been among the most financialized of all US corporations. The CEOs of these companies were among the IRA's most vocal critics. Merck was the first pharmaceutical company to sue the US government over the IRA-mandated price negotiations, arguing that this intervention was "tantamount to extortion" and violated its Fifth Amendment right that "requires the Government to pay 'just compensation' if it takes 'property' for public use" (Merck & Co. v. Xavier Becerra 2023). Pfizer's CEO Albert Bourla portrayed compliance with the provisions of the IRA as "negotiation with a gun to your head" (Singh 2023).

Merck began doing large-scale buybacks in the second half of the 1980s, and Pfizer in the first half of the 1990s. Merck sharply increased its buybacks in the late 1990s, and Pfizer even more so in the early 2000s. Over the 25-year period 1995–2019, Merck distributions to shareholders were 118 percent of net income, with 54 percent as buybacks. As CEO of Merck from January 1, 2011, to June 30, 2021, Kenneth Frazier averaged $27.4 million per year in TDC, of which 72 percent was stock-based. He remained as Merck chair until November 30, 2022, taking home $118.4 million in 2022, of which 97 percent was stock-based. During 2011–2022, the years in which Frazier was Merck CEO and chair, the company had $90.2 billion in net income, while it distributed $66.7 billion (equal to 74 percent of net income) as dividends and $46.4 billion (51 percent) as buybacks.

From 1995 through 2019, Pfizer distributed 114 percent of net income to shareholders, of which 58 percent were buybacks. Over his tenure as CEO from December 5, 2010, to January 1, 2019, Ian Read averaged $30.2 million per year in TDC, of which 64 percent was stock-based. Read stayed on as Pfizer executive chairman in 2019, pocketing another $49.7 million (89 percent stock-based) on his way to retirement. During 2011–2019, the years of Read's tenure as Pfizer CEO and chair, the company had $118.7 billion in net income, spending $63.9 billion (equal to 54 percent of net income) on dividends and $75.7 billion (64 percent) on buybacks.

A highly financialized corporation from the late 1980s, Pfizer committed to doing $8.9 billion in buybacks in early 2019, to be completed by August 1 of that year.[5]

---

[5] Pfizer's broker executed $2.1 billion in open-market repurchases in the first quarter of 2019 (ended March 31) but none thereafter. In addition, on February 7, 2019, Pfizer entered into a $6.8 billion "accelerated share repurchase" (ASR) agreement with Goldman Sachs. A device for stock-price manipulation, an ASR enables a company to reduce its shares outstanding by the full number of shares in the agreement on the date on which it signs the ASR contract. This arrangement gives an immediate, that is, "accelerated," boost to the company's earnings-per-share (EPS), without the company transgressing the limit under SEC Rule 10b-18 for the value of share repurchases that can be done on any single trading day. The bank (in this case Goldman

Table 5 Merck's distributions to shareholders as stock buybacks and cash dividends, in billions of current US dollars and as percent of net income, 1978–2022

Merck	Rev	NI	DV	BB	R&D	DV/NI	BB/NI	(DV+BB)/NI	R&D/Rev	BB/R&D	Employment	
			USD billion					%			EE 000S	% change
1978–1982	13.1	1.9	0.9	0.2	1.2	45	9	54	9	0.15	32.0	13.9
1983–1987	19.5	3.1	1.3	1.9	2.2	42	63	104	11	0.86	31.1	−2.8
1988–1992	38.4	8.6	3.9	2.0	4.4	45	23	68	11	0.46	38.4	235.0
1993–1997	85.6	17.0	7.9	7.7	6.9	47	45	92	8	1.12	53.8	40.1
1998–2002	199.5	32.4	14.0	16.7	12.5	43	52	95	6	1.34	77.3	43.7
2003–2007	114.8	25.0	16.5	6.5	20.8	66	26	92	18	0.31	59.8	−22.6
2008–2012	192.6	34.0	21.7	8.8	38.3	64	26	90	20	0.23	83.0	38.8
2013–2017	205.7	27.1	25.9	25.9	41.7	96	95	191	20	0.62	69.0	−16.9
2018–2022	245.1	50.7	30.7	16.0	59.0	61	32	92	24	0.27	69.0	0.0

Note: REV = revenues, NI = net income, BB = stock buybacks, DV = dividends, R&D = research & development expenditures

Source: Calculations from data in the S&P Compustat database and company 10-K reports.

Table 6 Pfizer's distributions to shareholders as stock buybacks and cash dividends, in billions of current US dollars and as percent of net income, 1978–2022

Pfizer	Rev	NI	DV	BB	R&D	DV/NI	BB/NI	(DV+BB)/NI %	R&D/REV	BB/R&D	Employment EE 000S	% change
	\multicolumn{5}{l	}{USD billion}							
1978–1982	14.8	1.3	0.6	0.0	0.8	46	0	46	5	0.00	40.0	−0.5
1983–1987	21.0	2.9	1.2	0.3	1.5	42	9	50	7	0.17	40.7	1.8
1988–1992	31.6	3.8	2.0	1.4	3.3	53	37	90	10	0.44	40.7	0.0
1993–1997	49.6	7.7	3.4	2.3	7.2	45	29	74	14	0.31	49.2	20.9
1998–2002	123.8	27.2	10.2	14.1	19.5	38	52	89	16	0.72	98.0	99.2
2003–2007	245.4	50.8	29.9	40.5	46.8	59	80	138	19	0.86	86.6	−11.6
2008–2012	292.5	49.6	32.9	18.7	43.0	66	38	104	15	0.44	91.5	5.2
2013–2017	255.4	66.6	35.1	37.5	38.9	53	56	109	15	0.96	90.2	−1.4
2018–2022	328.9	90.4	42.2	23.1	55.6	47	26	72	17	0.42	83.0	−8.0

Note: REV = revenues, NI = net income, BB = stock buybacks, DV = dividends, R&D = research & development expenditures

Source: Calculations from data in the S&P Compustat database and company 10-K reports.

After this buyback binge, however, the company ceased doing repurchases as it turned its strategic attention to conserving a portion of its profits to finance investment in its depleted drug pipeline. Previously, Pfizer's strategy had been to acquire other companies with lucrative drugs on the market that had years of patent life left and to extract the profits from these drugs to fund its distributions to shareholders. By the late 2010s, however, with Big Pharma acquisition targets unavailable and the patents on several of Pfizer's major drugs expiring, the board recognized that Pfizer itself could be taken over by another Big Pharma company unless it could develop high-revenue drugs internally.

For the sake of internal drug development, Pfizer refrained from doing buybacks from August 2019 through February 2022. Indeed, in an unusual move among US-based corporations, in January 2020, Pfizer publicly announced its commitment to forego buybacks that year, and it did so again in January 2021. The company did, however, increase its dividend every year from 2019 through 2023, paying 54 percent of net income over these five years. Also, Pfizer did $2 billion in buybacks in March 2022, timing these repurchases to give a manipulative boost to its sagging stock price. On March 1, Pfizer's stock price had sunk to $45.75 but, with the help of the $2 billion buyback, it was pumped up to $55.2 on April 8.

Stock Buybacks as the Enemy of Investment in Innovation

Pfizer's decision to cut back on buybacks followed the end of Ian Read's tenure as Pfizer CEO as of January 1, 2019, in favor of the current CEO, Albert Bourla. In an earnings call with stock-market analysts in January 2020, Bourla made an extraordinary admission of the company's financialized past, declaring that Pfizer had stopped doing buybacks so that the company could invest in innovation:

> The reason why in our capital allocation, we are allocating right now money [is] to increase the dividend and also to invest in our business ... all the CapEx to modernize our facilities. The reason why we don't do right now share repurchases, it is because we want to make sure that we maintain very strong firepower to invest in the business. The past was a very different Pfizer. The past of the last decade had to deal with declining of revenues, constant declining of revenues. And we had to do what we had to do even if that was financial engineering, purchasing back ourselves. We couldn't invest them and create higher value. Now it's a very different situation. We are a very different company. (Pfizer 2020)

Sachs) borrows the shares specified in the ASR agreement from asset funds that are not seeking to sell the shares. Then, during the life of the ASR agreement, the bank purchases the company's shares on the stock market in smaller amounts at its discretion at various points in time and returns the borrowed shares to the asset funds. In the case of Pfizer's 2019 $6.8 billion ASR, Goldman Sachs completed it on August 1, 2019.

Bourla did not explain why the "old" Pfizer – which, less than twelve months before, had done $8.9 billion in buybacks – "had to do what we had to do even if that was financial engineering, purchasing back ourselves." But his rambling statement to the analysts is a very rare recognition by a CEO of a major US-based corporation that stock buybacks are the enemy of investment in innovation.

Shortly thereafter, SARS-CoV-2 was declared a pandemic, and Pfizer found itself in what turned out to be a very lucrative partnership with BioNTech to develop, manufacture, and deliver the Covid-19 mRNA vaccine. Even though Pfizer's revenues almost doubled from $41.9 billion in 2020 to $81.3 billion in 2021, with profits soaring from $9.6 billion to $22 billion, the company refrained from doing buybacks, while the dividend payout ratio declined from 88 percent to 40 percent. In 2022, profits jumped further to $31.4 billion, bolstered by sales of Paxlovid (given emergency use authorization by the FDA in December 2021).

After executing $2 billion in buybacks in March 2022, Pfizer stated that the company "does not anticipate any additional share repurchases in 2022" (Pfizer 2022a). This self-restraint was probably based on its senior executives' recognition that, with the end of the pandemic in sight, Pfizer's windfall profits from its Covid-19 medicines were unlikely to last (Weber 2022). Indeed, in 2023, Pfizer's revenues plummeted from $100.3 billion to $58.5 billion, and its profits from $31.4 billion to $2.1 billion. Nevertheless, while still eschewing buybacks, in 2023 Pfizer raised its dividend payments to a record $9.2 billion – 436 percent of net income – the fourteenth straight year that its dividends went up.

Given the reliance of households as *shareholders* on yields from the stock market to fund big-ticket items such as college educations and retirements, one can accept that established business corporations, such as the pharmaceutical companies that we have been reviewing, should devote a portion of their profits to modest dividend payments. Medicare should, however, lower its MFP for companies that insist on paying excessive dividends.

Stock buybacks are different. Stock buybacks done as open-market repurchases only benefit corporate executives, Wall Street bankers, and hedge-fund managers who, as *sharesellers*, are in the business of timing the buying and selling of corporate stock. We have made the case that large-scale buybacks done as open-market repurchases should be banned (Lazonick 2023b; Lazonick and Tulum 2024). In this, we are not alone. At a press conference just prior to the passage of the IRA, which includes a (misguided and ineffectual) 1 percent tax on stock buybacks, Senate Majority Leader Chuck Schumer made his position clear:

> I hate stock buybacks. I think they are one of the most self-serving things that corporate America does. Instead of investing in workers and in training and in

research and in equipment, they don't do a thing to make their company better and they artificially raise the stock price by just reducing the number of shares. They're despicable. I'd like to abolish them. (Burns and Karl Evers-Hillstrom 2022)

In setting its MFP, Medicare should demand that the companies concerned cease doing buybacks. If a company insists on doing buybacks, the CMS should insist on a commensurately lower MFP. The companies, for their part, will warn that any limits placed on distributions to shareholders will undermine the ability of the pharmaceutical companies to raise funds on the stock market to fund investment in drug innovation. The problem with this argument is that, contrary to conventional wisdom, established drug companies do not, as a rule, seek to raise funds on the stock market to finance investment in their productive capabilities. Their shareholders simply buy and sell outstanding shares on the stock market.

Take, for example, Merck, which was founded in 1891 and went public on the stock market in 1941. The last time Merck issued common stock on the public stock market was in 1952. Over the next seventy-one years, the company received $15.9 billion (of which $14.6 billion, 1994–2023) from employees as proceeds from stock-based pay (mainly the exercise of stock options) and, in 2000, $1.5 billion from a preferred share issue.

In the case of Pfizer, it did its initial public offering in 1942, raising $5.9 million (most of which was used to pay off debt, redeem preferred stock, and purchase the shares of a deceased stockholder) (Anonymous 1942). The company also did a secondary public stock issue in 1951, raising $29 million. From 1953 through 2023, Pfizer collected $19.3 billion ($18.7 billion in 1993–2023) when employees exercised their stock options.

Bristol Myers Squibb was founded in 1858 and went public on the stock market in 1928. As with Merck and Pfizer, the last time that BMS issued common shares on the public stock market was in 1952, when, as Bristol-Myers, it did a rights issue for $4.2 million. Over the next seventy-one years, the company received $5.5 billion (of which $4.8 billion, 1993–2023) from employees as proceeds from the exercise of stock options.

It is a myth, therefore, that, once profitable, established companies such as Merck, Pfizer, and BMS need high drug prices to induce public shareholders to fund investment in drug innovation. To the contrary, funds retained from profits represent the financial foundation for investment in productive capabilities. We have dubbed this corporate resource-allocation regime "retain-and-reinvest": the corporation retains both earnings and employees for the sake of reinvesting in innovative products.

The opposite of retain-and-reinvest is "downsize-and-distribute": The corporation downsizes its labor force and distributes corporate cash to shareholders. By reducing retained earnings, distributions to shareholders undermine that financial foundation. Indeed, companies often price gouge their customers, terminate workers, squeeze suppliers, sell assets, take on debt, and avoid taxes to increase the so-called "free cash flow" that can be devoted to buybacks and dividends (Lazonick et al. 2020; Lazonick 2023b). As we have seen, distributions to shareholders are often far more than 100 percent of net income, in some cases over decades. In short, for an established pharmaceutical company, far from functioning as a value-creating institution, the stock market is a value-extracting institution (Lazonick 2018; Lazonick and Shin 2020).

What about the bond market? Is it a value-creating or a value-extracting institution? It depends on how a particular corporation uses the money it borrows. As a source of finance, corporate debt can be a complement to retained earnings in support of a retain-and-reinvest strategy. Debt can, however, provide a source of finance to do stock buybacks, although corporations do not usually state explicitly that repurchases are the purpose of a debt issue. While it is beyond the scope of this Element to delve into the issue of why pharmaceutical companies take on debt, Table 7 reveals that for the decade 2013–2022, the 14 pharmaceutical companies in the S&P 500 Index (see Table 3) could have avoided twice the $186 billion in net new debt that they took on between January 1, 2013, and December 31, 2022, if they had refrained from doing buybacks. AbbVie, for example, could have added only $16 billion in debt rather than $48 billion had the company not repurchased $32 billion in shares. In the case of Pfizer, which is the only pharmaceutical company in Table 7 that reduced its debt over the decade, it had over $52 billion in debt at the end of 2019 but paid off over $16 billion over the next three years as it refrained from doing buybacks while it reaped the gains of its Covid-19 medicines.

"Maximizing Shareholder Value" Legitimizes "Downsize-and-Distribute"

The myth of the stock-market as a value-creating institution derives directly from the prevailing ideology that, for the sake of economic efficiency, a business corporation should be run to "maximize shareholder value" (MSV). The MSV argument, put forth by academic economists known as agency theorists, is that, of all the participants in a company, it is only shareholders who make risky investments in the firm without a guaranteed return and, hence, it is only shareholders who have a claim on the firm's profits, if they occur (Lazonick 2018, 2023b). The theory assumes that other stakeholders in the corporation, including workers,

Table 7 Debt and buybacks at pharmaceutical companies and for 478 companies in the S&P 500 Index. 2013–2022

Company	Ticker	Buybacks. 2013–2022 $b	Total debt as of 12/31, $b 2012	Total debt as of 12/31, $b 2022	2013–2022 debt change, $b	Buybacks/ debt change %
BMS	BMY	27	7	41	33	81
ABBVIE	ABBV	32	16	63	48	67
AMGEN	AMGN	50	27	39	12	404
MERCK & CO	MRK	42	21	31	10	415
J&J	JNJ	57	16	40	23	243
ELI LILLY	LLY	16	6	16	11	150
BAXTER	BAX	7	6	17	11	62
PFIZER	PFE	61	37	36	−2	−3,717
Biogen	BIIB	28	1	7	5	512
Gilead Sciences	GILD	36	8	25	17	212
Viatris	VTRS	2	6	20	14	15
Regeneron	REGN	13	0	3	2	578
VERTEX	VRTX	3	1	1	0	1,500
Incyte	INCY	0	0	0	0	0
TOTAL 14 PHARMA		373	152	337	186	201
TOTAL 478 in S&P500		6,368	3,429	6,913	3,484	183
ASTRAZENECA	AZN	0	10	29	19	0
NOVARTIS	NVS	47	20	26	6	729
NOVO NORDISK	NVO	21	0	4	4	582

Sources: S&P Compustat database and company 10-K and 20-F reports.

receive guaranteed prices (e.g., employee's wages) for their productive contributions. Agency theory, however, overstates the risks borne by shareholders in making corporate investments, while ignoring risky investments by workers and taxpayers in productive resources that can enable business corporations to generate revenues and profits (Lazonick 2017, 2021).

Public shareholders do not, as a rule, invest directly in the firm. Rather, once a corporation is publicly listed, households, corporations, governments, and civil-society organizations, directly or indirectly through asset managers, become shareholders by purchasing shares outstanding on the stock market. In placing their funds in shares listed on a highly liquid stock market such as the New York Stock Exchange or NASDAQ, public shareholders take little risk; they enjoy limited liability if they hold the shares, and, given the liquidity of the stock market, at any instant and at a very low transaction cost, they can sell the shares at the going market price.

Through government investments in human capabilities and physical infrastructure, taxpayers regularly provide productive resources to companies without a guaranteed return. A formidable example is the spending on life-science research by the National Institutes of Health (NIH) with a 2024 budget of $47.3 billion (NIH 2024a, 2024b, 2024c). Businesses that make use of NIH-sponsored research benefit from the public knowledge that it generates. As risk-bearers, taxpayers who fund investments in such research, or in physical infrastructure such as roads, have a claim on resulting corporate profits, if they are generated. Through the tax system, governments, representing households as taxpayers, seek to extract this return from corporations that make profitable use of government investment in human capabilities and physical infrastructure.

No matter what corporate tax rate prevails, however, households as taxpayers face the uncertainty that changes in technological, market, and/or competitive conditions may prevent enterprises from generating profits and the related business tax revenues that serve as a return on the household taxpayers' investments in human capabilities and physical infrastructure. Moreover, tax rates are politically determined; households as taxpayers face the political uncertainty that predatory value extractors may convince government policymakers that they will not be able to make value-creating investments unless they are given tax cuts or financial subsidies that will permit adequate profits. Households as taxpayers face the risk that politicians may be put in power who accede to these demands for predatory value extraction.

Through their skills and efforts, workers regularly make productive contributions to the companies for which they work that are beyond the levels required to lay claim to their current pay. They do so, however, without guaranteed returns (Lazonick 1990, 2019). Any employer who is seeking to generate a higher-quality, lower-cost product knows the profound difference in the productivity levels of those employees who just punch the clock to get their daily pay and those who are committed to supporting the company's goals of generating products that can compete in terms of quality and cost. An innovative company wants workers who apply their skills and efforts to organizational learning so that they can make enduring productive contributions – including those that will enable the development of the firm's next generation of high-quality, low-cost products.

For their part, in making these productive contributions, employees expect that they will be able to build their careers within the company, putting themselves in positions to reap future benefits at work and in retirement. Yet these potential careers and returns are not guaranteed. In fact, under the downsize-and-distribute resource-allocation regime that MSV ideology legitimizes, these careers and returns are generally undermined.

Workers, therefore, supply their skills and efforts to the process of generating innovative products that, if successful, could create value, but they take the risk that their endeavors could be in vain. Far from reaping expected gains in the form of higher remuneration, more job security, and better working conditions, employees could face cuts in pay and benefits, or even find themselves laid off. Even if the innovation process is successful, workers face the possibility that the institutional environment in which MSV prevails will empower corporate executives to cut some workers' wages and lay off other workers – all so that the value they helped to create can be redirected to shareholders, including the senior executives themselves with their copious stock-based pay as well as hedge-fund managers whose stock-trading strategies count buybacks as money in the bank (Lazonick and Shin 2020). In short, the corporate resource-allocation regime may transform from retain-and-reinvest to downsize-and-distribute, with devastating impacts on the realized gains that committed employees had expected and deserved.

Merck under Kenneth Frazier provides an illuminating example of a CEO who, by all appearances, would have liked to embrace a retain-and-reinvest resource-allocation regime, but who, spouting the need to satisfy shareholders as investors in innovation, in fact implemented a downsize-and-distribute regime. Frazier drew public attention when, in August 2017, he resigned from President Trump's American Manufacturing Council after Trump condoned the violence of white nationalists in Charlottesville, Virginia (Patients For Affordable Drugs 2024). The following year, *Harvard Business Review* published an interview with Frazier, using his quote "Businesses Exist to Deliver Value to Society" as the article's title (Ignatius 2018). In 2023, after Frazier had retired from Merck, Darren Walker, president of the Ford Foundation, included a conversation with Frazier in his book *From Generosity to Justice*, entitling the chapter "A CEO Speaks for Justice" (Walker 2023, ch. 8). Also that year, McKinsey & Co. posted a two-part podcast with Frazier, with the subtitle "The Former CEO and Executive Chairman of the Pharmaceutical Company Offers Candid Reflections on How Crises Tested His Commitment to Values – Both Merck's and His Own" (Malhotra and Kuiken 2023).

In the *Harvard Business Review* interview, Frazier states:

> While a fundamental responsibility of business leaders is to create value for shareholders, I think businesses also exist to deliver value to society. Merck has existed for 126 years; its individual shareholders have turned over countless times. But our salient purpose in the world is to deliver medically important vaccines and medicines that make a huge difference for humanity. The revenue and shareholder value we create are an imperfect proxy for the value we create for patients and society.

In his discussion with Walker, Frazier invokes the well-known stakeholder credo of the last member of the Merck family to head the company.

> I feel very fortunate to work for a company that has, as part of its own value set, a belief based on the concept articulated by our modern-day founder George W. Merck: "Medicine is for the people – not for the profits." We're not exempt from our responsibility to shareholders, but we've always had the point of view that one of the most important ideas is equity in health.

In response to Walker's question about whether social justice would come from business leaders "moving away from this relentless paradigm of shareholder value," Frazier replied, "I think the idea that a company's only social responsibility is to increase profits for the stockholders is incorrect . . . . [B]usinesses exist to serve society's needs, not simply those of shareholders; . . . we need to ensure that we are behaving and operating our businesses in a way that brings benefit back to society."

Nice sentiments. But how, in practice, did Frazier's resource-allocation decisions at Merck confront the dominance of MSV ideology? In the McKinsey podcast, Frazier recounts the challenges that he faced from 2011, when he became Merck CEO:

> In my first five years, revenue actually declined, which is not an easy way to manage a company. So we needed to make a decision, or I needed to make a decision, to significantly reduce our expense base. That was probably the hardest thing I ever did as CEO because that implied laying off more than 10,000 loyal, committed people who deserved better. But we needed to do that in order to be able to invest in R&D, and also to be able to convince investors to be willing to continue to give us the capital necessary to do the long-term R&D play that we wanted to do. So, we took about $3 billion of cost out of the base. We ended up with a very successful cancer drug called Keytruda. Had we not freed up that capital, we would not have been able to invest as strongly in Keytruda.

In 2011, Merck's revenues were a then-record $48 billion, but they declined steadily to $39.5 billion in 2015. Over those five years, Merck's employment declined from 94,000 to 68,000, while R&D spending, which had increased from $5.8 billion in 2009 to $11 billion in 2010, fell to $6.7 billion in 2015. What Frazier does not say in any of the three interviews (perhaps because he is never asked) is that in 2011–2015 Merck distributed $25.7 billion in dividends, equal to 77 percent of net income and $22.9 billion in buybacks, another 69 percent of income.

Given the net reduction of employment of 26,000 over these five years, that works out to *$988,000 in dividends and $881,000 in buybacks per job lost.* The employment of "loyal, committed people who deserved better," as Frazier describes those laid off, was sacrificed on the altar of MSV. Frazier's response is that he had to "convince investors to be willing to continue to give us the capital necessary to do the long-term R&D play that we wanted to do." As we have seen, however, the last time that Merck went to public shareholders to raise funds for investment was in 1952! So, who are these "investors" to whom Merck had to distribute $48.6 billion as dividends and buybacks in 2011–2015? Perhaps, Frazier is referring to Merck employees, including senior executives, who paid the company $4.9 billion in exercising stock options. With the distributions to shareholders, those "investors" stood to realize more gains on their stock-based pay – at the expense of about 30 percent of Merck employees who lost their jobs (and perhaps their unvested stock options or stock awards).

In the end, what saved Merck under Frazier was Keytruda's approval as a cancer immunotherapy. The drug was originally developed by Organon, a pharmaceutical company that had been founded in the Netherlands in 1923, which Schering-Plough acquired in 2007. Two years later, Merck gained control of Keytruda when it merged with Schering-Plough. Approved by the FDA in 2014, by 2023 the blockbuster drug reached over $25 billion in sales, 42 percent of all Merck revenues (see Figure 4).

In his *Harvard Business Review* interview, Frazier mentions that Keytruda has a list price of $150,000 for a year's supply and asks, rhetorically, "Why is that the right price?" The CEO contends that Merck's general pricing policy asks: "How should we price [a new medicine] to get the adoption curve we want?" He answers that the company wants to set a price that "patients and the

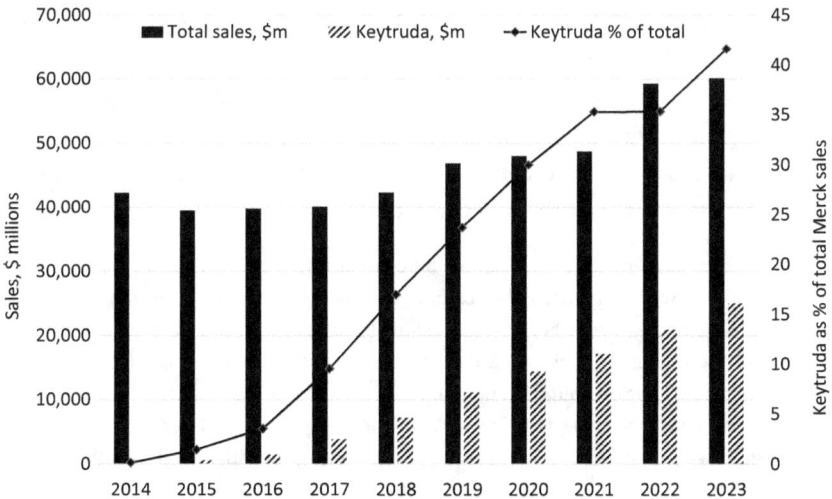

Figure 4 Merck's annual sales of Keytruda, in current dollars and as percentages of Merck's total sales, 2014–2023

Source: Merck 10-K filings with the Securities and Exchange Commission [healthcare] system can afford," which must be balanced with "providing a good return to our shareholders – because they keep financing the research that will produce tomorrow's drugs."

CMS take note. Shareholders do not finance the research that will produce tomorrow's drugs. Households as workers and taxpayers do, and they, not shareholders, are the participants in the corporation that MFP should incentivize and reward.

The Illogic (and Immorality) of "Value-based Pricing"

Besides legitimizing predatory value extraction, the dominance of MSV as an ideology of corporate resource allocation distorts the perspectives of pharmaceutical executives on what constitutes a "fair" drug price. If, of all stakeholders in society, only shareholders "create value," then it may seem like a logical next step to argue that the "fair" price of the product is one which enables the company's shareholders to capture all the value to society of an innovative drug – that is, "value-based pricing."[6]

Here is a "horse's mouth" example of the argument for "value-based pricing" as put forth by Albert Bourla, CEO of Pfizer, one of the companies with which Medicare is negotiating IRA-mandated MFP. In this case, the medicine in question was the Covid-19 vaccine that Pfizer had developed with Germany-based BioNTech. The US government agreed to pay $20 per dose for the BioNTech/Pfizer vaccine. In writing a book on Pfizer's role in securing emergency use authorization for the vaccine, Bourla is very explicit concerning why, in the context of a worldwide pandemic, he was willing to accept $20 per dose as a fair price (Bourla 2022).

Bourla begins his account of Pfizer's role in the price-setting process by making a general statement concerning value-based pricing: "The way we price our medicines is by calculating the value they bring to patients, to the healthcare system, and to society." The CEO continues:

> For example, if one hundred people take a heart medicine and as a result we have five fewer heart attacks, we calculate the cost that these five heart attacks would generate to the healthcare system (ambulance rides, hospital stays, tests, doctors, caregivers, work days lost, etc.) and compare it to the cost of the medicine for one hundred people.
>
> We could price the vaccine at $600 per dose, and still the healthcare system would pay less than it saves – not counting the value of human lives

---

[6] Arguments concerning who should capture "value to society" then seek to measure what that value to society is. In this Element, we refrain from entering this debate because we are putting forth a much broader set of arguments about value creation ("value for society") and its relation to value extraction (supported by arguments, often false, about "value to society").

saved. I realized that this could become a gigantic financial opportunity for us but also that in the middle of a pandemic we could not use the standard value calculation for setting the price. I asked for a different approach.

Bourla goes on to say that he instructed Pfizer's pricing team "to bring me the current cost of other cutting-edge vaccines like for measles, shingles, pneumonia, etc." Their response:

> In the US they were priced between $150 and $200 per dose. It sounded fair to me to match the low end of the already existing vaccine prices. No one could say that we were using the pandemic as an opportunity to set prices at unusually high levels. I told my team to begin procurement discussions at this starting point and offer discounts for volume commitments.

Bourla then recounts that, even with a price that was one-quarter to one-third of his value-based price of $600, "a level of discomfort started gnawing at me . . . that we might be missing an opportunity to gain something more valuable than a fair financial return."

> We had a chance to gain back our industry's reputation, which had been under fire for the last two decades. In the US, pharmaceuticals ranked near the bottom of all sectors, right next to the government, in terms of reputation.

Note that, in these statements, Bourla recognizes that even a fraction of the "value-based price" would still provide Pfizer with "a fair financial return" but would be a price that would further sully the poor reputation of the pharmaceutical industry. The CEO's "level of discomfort" led him to go back to the Pfizer pricing team, requesting the current prices of the *cheapest commodity vaccines* as a possible benchmark for pricing the Covid-19 vaccine. Bourla was informed that "[t]heir low end is around $20 to $30." He then told the pricing team: "We are changing course . . . . For the high-income countries, the starting point should be the low end of flu pricing. We can still offer discounts for high-volume commitments." Bourla then remarks that, for marketing purposes, $20 per dose could be construed as "the cost of a simple meal, not a cutting-edge vaccine."

The pandemic is over, and the returns are in. At $20 per dose, with the profits shared 50:50 with BioNTech, Pfizer got more than a "fair financial return" from its participation in the development, manufacture, and delivery of the Covid-19 vaccine, Comirnaty. In 2021 and 2022, Pfizer recorded sales of $36.7 billion and $37.8 billion, respectively, of Comirnaty, with total corporate net income of $22 billion and $31.4 billion, up from $16.3 billion in 2019 and $9.6 billion in 2020.

Taking into account Pfizer's huge profits from its antiviral Covid-19 pill Paxlovid (which it sold to the US government at $530 per course), we estimate that Pfizer's profits from Comirnaty for 2021 and 2022 combined were $9 billion, at the "simple meal" price of $20. That is a nice profit for a product that Pfizer could sell with emergency use authorization, limits on liability, government-guaranteed procurement contracts, and the profits of which the company had to share with BioNTech. At the "cutting edge vaccine" price of $150, Pfizer's profits from Comirnaty for the two years would have been about $45 billion, while at the "value-based" price of $600, profits would have been about $270 billion.

If that is an example of what a company such as Pfizer considers to be a "fair financial return," public disdain for the people who run the pharmaceutical companies would seem to be well deserved. It may be that the value to society of the BioNTech/Pfizer Covid-19 vaccine was $270 billion, or even much more. For decades prior to the pandemic, however, teams of scientists around the world had engaged in foundational and translational research that made it possible to develop manufacture, and deliver an mRNA-based Covid-19 vaccine in 2021 and 2022 (Tulum et al. 2021; Tulum and Lazonick 2024). What "fair" claim does Pfizer (or for that matter Germany-based BioNTech, which was the partner that actually formulated the vaccine) have to even consider demanding a price that would capture its value to society?

As a corporation in the business of developing, manufacturing, and delivering medicines, all that should matter to Pfizer is that, in its participation in those processes to make doses of Comirnaty available, the company will generate sufficient profits to reward its employees who helped create those profits, pay its corporate taxes, distribute reasonable dividends to shareholders, and retain sufficient earnings to reinvest in drug innovation. In conjunction with MSV ideology, "value-based pricing" is pharma CEO code for claiming that the company's shareholders have a right set a price at whatever level the CEO and the board see fit – and give all or more of the profits back to themselves. Then, as in Bourla's "simple meal" analogy, a lower drug price is portrayed as a concession to society for which the company is sacrificing its "fair financial return" – and for we should all be profoundly and profusely grateful.

Meanwhile, over at Merck, CEO Frazier had his own thoughts about value-based pricing, as an extension of his discussion of the price of Keytruda, as put forth in his 2018 interview in *Harvard Business Review* (Ignatius 2018). In providing a more detailed justification of the pricing of Keytruda, Frazier, like Bourla, takes value-based pricing as his ideological starting point, but then recognizes other factors related to affordability and reinvestment in innovation that actually guide his thinking about the price that should be charged. As he puts it in the interview:

> First of all, we're talking about a life-and-death situation. For people who are suffering and bereft of hope, we can actually make a difference. Then there's

the cost to the system of not treating cancer. Data shows that a 10% reduction in cancer deaths would have a huge positive impact on society economically – far and above the cost of Keytruda. We're saving society money in that respect. And consider the financial model of the pharmaceutical business: The price of this successful drug is paying for the 90%-plus projects that fail. We can't have winners if we can't pay for losers.

Frazier goes on to say that Merck tempers the high price of Keytruda by recognizing "our obligation to help make sure that people who need these medicines have meaningful access to them, and we've provided Keytruda to thousands of patients at no cost." He also makes the claim that "the full cost of the drugs we sell doesn't come back to Merck." He explains:

> On average, 30% of it goes to others in the supply chain: insurers, governments, distributors, hospitals. But you're right, a lot of the public concern is about the cost to the patient. And that has to do in part with the design of insurance benefits. An in-network patient might pay roughly 3% of the medical bill but would pay about 15% for pharmaceuticals in copay and coinsurance. We negotiate substantial rebates and discounts with large payers, but often they aren't passed on to the patient. If you have to pay that much money, the arguments I've made are not going to please you.

An analysis of which actors in the pharmaceutical supply chain, including PBMs, benefit from the price of a drug will require a separate study. What is germane here is that Frazier enumerates various practical considerations that influence the product's price. But, like Pfizer's Bourla, Frazier has bought into the ideology that the value-based price is what the pharmaceutical company, that is, its shareholders, should be getting. In the *Harvard Business Review* interview, the magazine's senior editor Adi Ignatius asks Frazier: "How does the trend toward outcomes-based [i.e., value-based] pricing in the healthcare industry affect Merck?" Frazier's response:

> I think it's a good thing. Society can spend only so much money on health care, so we have to spend it wisely. It's important that we spend it on things that are actually creating value and having an impact. That's what outcomes-based pricing is all about.

In this statement, Frazier assumes that, because society prioritizes a certain type of drug research based on its value for society, the pharmaceutical company that sells an approved drug that results from that research should capture all, or even a substantial portion, of that value to society, in an "outcomes-based" price.

In practice, the argument for value-based pricing for the sake of MSV is just an ideological device for asserting that the pharmaceutical company's senior executives have the exclusive right to determine what that drug price should be.

When the company charges a price that is lower than its value to society, so the argument goes, its shareholders are, for the benefit of society, sacrificing the "value to society" that they have a right to capture.

Perhaps CEO Frazier really believes that Merck's shareholders fund Merck's investments in innovation. What Frazier does not consider is the long history of collective and cumulative learning in foundational, translational, and clinical research that makes a product like Keytruda possible. Over the course of decades, the vast majority of scientists and other personnel involved in CCL have done their jobs, perhaps with some hope that eventually they would help to create value for society, but with their pay determined by their educational qualifications, career experience, commitment to their work, and, perhaps to some extent, the priority that society has placed on the work that they are doing. But normal, hardworking people, even those with elevated educational credentials, do not negotiate prices for their labor that reflect value to society – only in part because, when they do their work, its ultimate value to society in terms of safe and effective medicines cannot be known.

Given the communities of scientists and those who assist them in their work who contribute to social value creation, why should the company that markets the drug assume that it is the party that should be first in line in capturing the value to society of that drug? Indeed, what enables value creators even in the company to benefit from value to society when all the company's profits and more are being distributed to shareholders – who, by the way, play virtually no role in the value-creation process?

We submit that value-based pricing, as advocated by senior pharmaceutical executives, is an idea that could only be put in practice in a world that buys into the ideology that, for the sake of value to society, a business corporation should be run to maximize shareholder value. As elaborated at length elsewhere, it is an ideology based on a theory of how to extract value from society rather than about how to create value for society (Lazonick 2021). The irrelevance of MSV as a theory of value creation becomes apparent when we consider, as we do in the next two sections of the Element, the roles of foundational and translational research in making possible the ten MFP drugs in the first round of IRA-mandated negotiations.

3 Foundational, Translational, and Clinical Research
The Pivotal Role of NIH Funding

The National Institutes of Health (NIH), the largest public funder of biomedical research in the world, has played a pivotal role in the development of drugs for the treatment or prevention of diseases. As mentioned earlier, from 1938 through 2023, the NIH spent over $1.6 trillion in 2023 dollars on life-science research and had a 2024 operating budget of $47.2 billion (NIH 2024b). Over the decades, NIH has been at the epicenter of a life-sciences ecosystem in which, through CCL of scientific communities engaged in foundational, translational, and clinical research, business corporations gain access to knowledge and capabilities that are indispensable to the development, manufacture, and delivery of safe and effective drugs.

NIH-funded research has led to significant advancements in various drug treatments, including the development of the first statin drugs for lowering cholesterol, which have revolutionized the management of cardiovascular disease. Additionally, NIH-funded research has resulted in the discovery of the first ACE inhibitors for treating high blood pressure, greatly improving the outcomes of hypertensive patients. The development of the first monoclonal antibodies for treating cancer emerged from NIH-funded research, providing hope for patients with previously untreatable malignancies.

In recent years, the US government has recognized the importance of continued investment in drug R&D. The 21st Century Cures Act of 2016 allocated an additional $6.3 billion in funding for the NIH over ten years. This substantial investment has enabled the NIH to support research on a wide range of diseases, including Alzheimer's, cancer, and diabetes, with the aim of developing innovative treatments and cures. According to United for Medical Research (2024), in 2023, "the $37.81 billion NIH awarded to researchers in the 50 U.S. states and the District of Columbia supported 412,041 jobs and $92.89 billion in economic activity." This government spending provides a solid, and one could argue indispensable, foundation of knowledge for the R&D activities of the corporate members of PhRMA, which spent an estimated total of $101 billion on R&D in 2022 (PhRMA 2024b).

Enabling the discovery and development of the ten MFP drugs was a remarkable transformation in the field of medicine. Researchers at Bentley University's Center for Integration of Science and Industry, led by Fred Ledley, have documented the role of government-funded applied research in the value-creation process that resulted in the development of the ten MFP drugs, shown in Tables 1 and 2 (Zhou et al. 2024). Based on extensive analysis of NIH grants, publications, patents, and clinical trials, the Bentley study finds that the NIH invested $11.7 billion in research leading to the approval of the ten MFP drugs. This early public investment averaged $895.4 million per drug, resulting in an estimated $1.485 billion per drug savings for the pharmaceutical industry, on a par with their own reported investment levels.

Breakthroughs in Foundational Science That Have Transformed Drug Discovery

In *Science–The Endless Frontier*, published in 1945, Vannevar Bush, a prominent American engineer and science administrator, propounded the critical importance for industrial development of government investment in basic research (Bush and Holt 2021). He recognized that basic, or what we call foundational, research, which is performed without a focus on a specific application, can lead to transformative technologies and unexpected uses that have the potential to revolutionize value creation in a range of industrial sectors. Through various government agencies, the United States implemented Bush's "endless frontier" vision in the postwar decades, supporting knowledge creation through both foundational and translational science.

Foundational research provides the basic scientific knowledge for understanding the natural world, particularly biological systems, without an immediate focus on practical applications. Translational research builds upon this foundational knowledge, aiming to bridge the gap between laboratory discoveries and patient care. It encompasses activities that lead to new drug discovery and preclinical research, including identifying, validating, and optimizing new molecular leads, and, in later stages, it involves clinical research where the selected new leads are tested on humans through rigorous drug trials to evaluate their safety and efficacy.

Foundational research enhances the productivity of translational research by providing the fundamental insights that enable identification of new drug targets and therapeutic approaches. Breakthroughs in foundational science can also lead to the development of new research tools and technologies that facilitate translation of knowledge into clinical applications. Translational research, in turn, improves the efficiency of clinical research by providing well-characterized drug candidates with a higher probability of success in human trials, which themselves depend on advances in statistical and computational methods.

This interconnectedness highlights the importance of a continuous feedback loop between these stages such that even information derived from inconclusive clinical research creates a vantage point for further foundational and translational research. That is, unknowns exposed through product development pose new challenges for the scientific communities engaged in foundational and translational research. It is through collective and cumulative learning that teams of scientists engage in the perpetual cycle of knowledge creation and refinement within the biopharma science ecosystem, linking foundational, translational, and clinical research.

Since the 1990s, foundational research in biology and other fields of science and technology have been transforming the possibilities for translational research to pursue drug discovery and clinical research to engage in drug development. Enabled by breakthroughs in basic science during this period, the evolution of drug discovery has seen a significant shift, moving from serendipitous findings to a more rational and targeted approach, as shown in Table 8.

In phenotypic drug discovery (PDD), scientists observe the effects of compounds on whole organisms or cells without a predefined molecular target. While capable of identifying potential drugs, this approach often faces challenges in understanding the mechanisms involved and ways to optimize their efficacy (Bartfai and Lees 2006). The advent of target-based drug discovery (TDD) revolutionized this process, focusing on identifying specific biological targets involved in disease and designing drugs to modulate their activity. More recently, structure-based drug design (SDD) has emerged as a powerful tool, utilizing the three-dimensional structure of the target to design highly specific and potent drugs (Callaway 2015).

Characterizing these distinct approaches are focus, the primary point of attention or emphasis in the research process, and specific methods or techniques used to achieve the research goal. PDD is often the starting point for drug discovery, as it can identify compounds with therapeutic potential even when the underlying mechanisms are unclear. While TDD centers on identifying a specific biological target, such as a protein or enzyme, involved in a disease process, SDD utilizes the three-dimensional structure of the biological target to design drugs that fit and bind to the target with high specificity and affinity.

PDD's advancements have stemmed mainly from life sciences and biotechnology, with high-throughput screening (HTScr) and cell culture techniques allowing for efficient testing of compounds. TDD's progress has been driven by a deeper understanding of biology, biochemistry, and the advent of recombinant DNA technology, enabling the identification and manipulation of specific targets (Watson 1990). SDD emerged from advancements in physics and chemistry, particularly X-ray crystallography and NMR spectroscopy, which have provided insights into protein structures, while computational chemistry facilitated drug design based on these structures (Zheng et al. 2015; Blundell 2017). Enabling all these methods of drug discovery have been advances in information-and-communication technologies (ICT) since the 1960s.

The advent of transistors, second-generation (mainframe) computers, and robotic tools inspired scientists to introduce emerging computer technology in the discovery and design of innovative new drugs as early as the 1960s and 1970s. This new approach permitted high-throughput screening (HTScr), with

Table 8 Phenotypic drug discovery (PDD), target-based drug discovery (TDD), structure-based drug discovery (SDD)

Feature	Phenotypic drug discovery (PDD)	Target-based drug discovery (TDD)	Structure-based drug discovery (SDD)
Focus	Whole organism/cell phenotype	Specific biological target	3D structure of the target
Methods	High-throughput screening, phenotypic assays	Target validation, lead optimization	Virtual screening, structure-based optimization
Starting point	Disease model	Known target	Known target structure
Limitations	Difficult target identification, potential for off-target effects	May overlook non-target-based candidates	Requires detailed target structure, computationally intensive
Example (anticoagulants)	Warfarin, phenprocoumon (early discovery)	Apixaban, rivaroxaban (later development)	Apixaban, rivaroxaban (optimization)
Key scientific and technological advancements	High-throughput screening (1980s–present), cell culture techniques (1950s–present)	Molecular biology (1950s–present), genomics (1990s–present), recombinant DNA technology (1970s–present)	X-ray crystallography (1910s–present), NMR spectroscopy (1940s–present), computational chemistry (1980s–present)
Domain of origin	Primarily life sciences and biotechnology	Life sciences and biotechnology, biochemistry	Physics, chemistry, computer science
Emergence	Early twentieth century	1980s–1990s	1990s–present

Sources: See Appendix 1 for Table 8 references

pharmaceutical companies digitizing their large libraries of chemical compounds. Scientists can then screen the libraries to identify compounds for specific medical interventions. Government-funded initiatives such as the NIH's Molecular Libraries Program (MLP launched in 2004), HTScr, and combinatorial chemistry, which saw significant advances in the 1980s and 1990s, enabled rapid screening of vast chemical libraries for potential drug candidates, enhancing the power of PDD (Inglese et al. 2007). Advances in bioinformatics and computational biology, supported by initiatives at the NIH's National Center for Biotechnology Information (NCBI) (established in 1988), allowed for the prediction of drug targets and their interactions with potential drugs, streamlining the drug discovery process, and accelerating the transition from PDD to TDD (Sayers et al. 2022).

In the 1990s, the exponential enhancement of the computing power of silicon chips gave rise to the computer-aided drug design revolution. The first-generation supercomputers enabled high-throughput sequencing (HTSeq) that improved the pace and cost of the gene-mapping process, drastically increasing the efficiency of utilizing genomic data. Simultaneously, developments in molecular biology and genomics, fueled by the Human Genome Project (completed in 2003) and subsequent government-funded research mainly through the NIH – the funding of which doubled in real terms between 1998 and 2004 – provided deeper insights into disease mechanisms and potential therapeutic targets (Watson 1990; Collins 2001; Sampat 2012). Techniques like polymerase chain reaction (PCR) (Kornberg 1995), developed in the 1980s, and DNA sequencing, continually refined with government support, enabled the identification of genetic variations associated with diseases, paving the way for the transition from TDD to SDD (Ashley 2016).

While the concept of SDD originated in the 1960s, its practical implementation was limited by the technology of the time. It was only in the later decades, with the convergence of various scientific and technological advancements in the 1980s and 1990s, that SDD gradually became a powerful tool for designing effective drugs. Advancements in X-ray crystallography, NMR spectroscopy, and computational modeling allowed scientists to visualize the 3D structures of proteins as biological targets and design drugs that specifically interact with and modulate these targets (Petsko 2003). This approach led to the development of successful drugs, including HIV protease inhibitors and direct factor Xa inhibitors (Nar 2012; Venkatraman 2012; Zheng et al. 2023).

Protein design is one of the early applications of artificial intelligence (AI)-based machine learning programs that are powered by the latest generation of supercomputers, equipped with advanced electronic circuits. Characterized by the latest stage of convergence in the fields of ICT and biotechnology, since the early 2000s AI-supported genomics and proteomics research that further enhances drug discovery and development processes has been ushering in the intelligent medicines revolution (IMR). Further AI advances have enabled high-throughput proteomics (HTPro), permitting large-scale analysis of proteins to gain insight into their structures and functions (Cui et al. 2022).

IMR is a possibility because of a long history of knowledge accumulation and technological innovation that are in the public domain. Of great importance are advances in protein engineering and structural biology, including X-ray crystallography, nuclear magnetic resonance (NMR) spectroscopy, and cryogenic electron microscopy (cryo-EM), often supported by grants from agencies such as the NIH. These tools facilitate the design of drugs that specifically interact with target proteins. These technologies have collectively enabled the development of new drug classes, offering improved treatment options for a wide range of diseases.

Transformation of Drug Discovery and Its Impact on the Productivity of Drug R&D

PDD can reveal novel targets and therapies, but it has drawbacks. Identifying the molecular target responsible for a phenotypic change can be a time-consuming and complex process, often resulting in drugs with multiple targets or unknown mechanisms of action. The transition from phenotypic to target-based and structure-based drug discovery, however, led to a perceived "productivity crisis" in the early 2000s, characterized by increased R&D costs, longer development timelines, and high attrition rates (Scannell et al. 2012).

The long-term impact of this transformation is still unfolding, but it clearly has shifted the paradigm toward more rational drug design, potentially leading to greater efficiency and success in the future, despite the ongoing challenges of high costs and complex diseases. As drug discovery approaches maturity, the industry is witnessing a gradual improvement in clinical trial success rates and the development of more targeted and effective therapies.

At AstraZeneca, for example, molecules that progressed from the preclinical stage all the way through Phase III clinical trials declined from 9 percent of all candidates in the 1990s to 4 percent in 2009. In 2010, AstraZeneca scientists embarked on an investigation of internal R&D operations to explore why the company's R&D productivity often ranked below the industry average (Cook et al. 2014). Based on inquiries into the company's internal learning process, AstraZeneca scientists discovered that many lead compounds that the company scientists selected for clinical studies based on their varying degrees of pharmacologic effects failed during the human trials due to safety reasons.

The report concluded that the lack of biological insight into disease pathways and mechanisms of action were the primary reason for the lackluster performance of the company's drug discovery and development process. Under Pascal Soriot, who became CEO in 2013, AstraZeneca underwent a major transformation, resulting in a remarkable expansion of the company's product pipeline and portfolio over the subsequent decade (Morgan et al. 2018; Tulum et al. 2023). The company achieved this successful transformation by embarking on a new learning strategy that entailed enhancing the depth and breadth of organizational learning in biology (Tulum et al. 2023).

4 Collective and Cumulative Learning in Translational Research

Translational-Research Enablers of Clinical Research

The opponents of direct price negotiations under the IRA contend that pharmaceutical companies shoulder significant financial risks associated with drug development. Therefore, they argue that the companies should reap any commercial benefits resulting from drug innovation. In a *Health Affairs* analysis of the ten MFP drugs, McElwee et al. (2024) oppose the price regulations under IRA by categorically dismissing the importance of taxpayer support as a determinant of a maximum fair price, given that foundational research supported by government funding as well as certain aspects of translational research (a) are NOT directly relevant to the drug discovery or development process, (b) have impacts on these processes that are impossible to measure, and (c) have no value in the absence of business-sector investments in clinical research that transforms discoveries resulting from foundational research into commercially viable medicinal products.

Dismissed in the *Health Affairs* analysis is the government support for translational research that has enabled scientists to enhance their understanding of intricate biological processes at the molecular level. By acquiring insights into *biological pathways* and *mechanisms of action*, scientists could begin to describe and explain the biological processes that lead to specific biological outcomes. Many diseases are caused by disruptions in biological pathways. Drugs often work by targeting specific molecules or steps within these pathways, thus eliminating disruptions. Hence, research into biological pathways is a crucial part of TDD and SDD approaches.

Biological pathway refers to a series of actions among molecules in a cell that leads to a certain product or a change in the cell. A pathway can control various processes in the body, including metabolism (how your body breaks down food and nutrients for energy); gene expression (how your genes are turned on or off, influencing your traits and characteristics); and signal transduction (how cells communicate with each other to coordinate bodily functions). Insight into biological pathways involves identifying the key components (e.g., genes, proteins, enzymes) and their roles in the biological process. It is like describing the steps to follow in a cake recipe during the baking process.

Mechanism of action elucidates the underlying principles and causal relationships that drive the biological process. This science goes beyond simply describing the steps in the process by delving into the how and why of each interaction, which is like understanding the chemical reactions that occur during the process of baking the cake.

Comprehension of a drug's mechanism of action and the biological pathways that it influences is paramount in the realm of drug discovery. It empowers scientists to pinpoint potential drug targets – specific molecules or processes implicated in a disease. By modulating these targets through a drug, a therapeutic effect can be achieved. Identifying and validating targets, confirming their relevance to the disease, constitute crucial steps in the drug development process. This knowledge serves as a guiding light in the design of novel drugs, which significantly increase the likelihood of developing safe and effective treatments.

While a deep understanding of biological mechanisms is essential for targeted drug discovery, the journey from initial insight to approved therapy is often long and winding, involving collective learning by communities of scientists that cumulates over time. Sustained government support plays a crucial role in this CCL as the ability to identify and validate drug targets relies heavily on foundational knowledge generated through basic-science research. Government funding agencies, most notably the NIH, have been instrumental in supporting this research, laying the groundwork for the development of many new medicines in recent decades, including the ten MFP drugs subject to price negotiations under IRA. While the high cost of technology maturation is often cited as a justification for high drug prices, policymakers, such as those involved in Medicare price negotiations, need to consider this public contribution and strive for a pricing model that incentivizes innovation while ensuring affordable access to lifesaving medicines.

The process of translating new discoveries in biological processes into novel drugs, however, involves a lengthy and expensive technology maturation phase, often requiring decades of research and development. Government support, particularly in the early stages when extreme uncertainty renders investment by pharmaceutical companies scarce, is crucial for bridging the gap between foundational research and commercialization. For instance, a study by Ledley and colleagues reveals a significant lag, averaging 44 years, between the initiation of technology and the approval of 138 cancer drugs utilizing that technology (McNamee and Ledley 2017). In another study, they document long lead times in drug development, averaging 36 years, between the initiation of new research areas and the first drug approvals, based on the analysis of over 400 new molecular entities (Beierlein et al. 2017).[7]

While confirming that commitment to pharmaceutical innovation is a long-term endeavor, the Ledley studies document the sustained government support required for the development of foundational-research and translational-research enablers of clinical research. The government often extends this support to the finance of clinical trials, regulatory approval processes, and post-marketing surveillance, which also drive the overall cost of drug development. Government funding and incentives, such as tax credits and expedited review processes, can help de-risk these stages and accelerate the availability of new treatments. Moreover, the collaborative nature of drug development, involving academic institutions, civil-society organizations, government agencies, and business corporations, necessitates a robust public infrastructure for knowledge sharing, data collection, and regulatory oversight. Government support facilitates this collective effort, creating the possibilities that, cumulatively, scientific advancements translate into safe and effective therapies that benefit patients and society as a whole.

The cases of the ten Medicare-negotiated drugs exemplify the interconnectedness of foundational research, translational research, and clinical research, potentially culminating in pharmaceutical innovation. These drugs, which have significantly reduced healthcare costs and improved health benefits, would not have been possible without years of foundational research that provided the basic knowledge and technological tools for their development. Translational research then played a crucial role in adapting these foundational-research findings into practical therapies that could be tested and approved for use in patients. Pharmaceutical companies then took these therapies and invested in clinical trials and manufacturing processes to bring them to market.

By tracing the biological pathways and mechanisms of action that underpin the ten MFP drugs, we aim to demonstrate that the gains from innovation are not solely attributable to the clinical research efforts of pharmaceutical companies. Instead, they are the result of CCLs by a diverse array of actors, including people working in academic institutions, government agencies, civil-society organizations, and other business corporations.

For the first round of price negotiations, Medicare selected ten high-priced, single-source drugs from four therapeutic classes: anticoagulants, antidiabetics and/or cardiovasculars, disease-modifying antirheumatics (DMARDs), and anti-cancer drugs. As Table 9 shows, these drugs achieve their therapeutic goals by

---

[7] See also Mohs and Greig (2017), Sismondo (2017), Robinson (2017), and Roy (2023).

Table 9 Overview of drug class, mechanism of action, patent status, and approval history for Medicare's first ten MFP drugs

Brand name	Generic name	Initial patent	FDA approval	Path	Patentee/licensee	Therapeutic class	Mechanism of action
Eliquis	Apixaban	2004	2012	NDA	*DuPont (Rx unit)*	Anticoagulants	Direct factor Xa inhibitor
Xarelto	Rivaroxaban	2005	2011	NDA	Bayer		
NovoLog/ Fiasp	Insulin aspart	1982	2000/2017	BLA	Novo Nordisk	Antidiabetics and cardiovasculars	Human insulin analog
Januvia	Sitagliptin	2002	2006	NDA	Merck & Co.		DPP-4 inhibitor
Farxiga	Dapagliflozin	2003	2014	NDA	*Amylin*		SGLT2 inhibitor
Jardiance	Empagliflozin	2007	2014	NDA	Boehringer Ingelheim/Eli Lilly		
Entresto	Valsartan/ sacubitril	1995/2010	1996/2021	NDA	Ciba-Geigy		NEPinh/ARB
Enbrel	Etanercept	1989	1998	BLA	Roche/*Immunex*	Disease-modifying antirheumatics	TNF inhibitor
Stelara	Ustekinumab	2009	2009	BLA	*Medarex/Centocor*		IL-12/IL-23 inhibitor
Imbruvica	Ibrutinib	2007	2013	NDA	*Celera Genomics*	Anticancer	BTK inhibitor

Notes: **Path** = Drug regulatory approval path; **BLA** = Biologics license application; **ND** = New drug application. BMS acquired DuPont pharma unit in 2001; BMS acquired Amylin in 2012 under diabetes joint venture with AstraZeneca and in 2013 AstraZeneca acquired BMS' stake in the JV; Novartis was formed following the mergers of Ciba-Geigy and Sandoz in 1996; Amgen acquired Immunex in 2002; J&J acquired Centocor in 1999; BMS acquired Medarex in 2009; Pharmacyclics acquired the pharma product pipeline of Celera Genomics in 2006 before Quest Diagnostics acquired the company in 2011.

Sources: Authors' own analysis based on company annual filings and other public sources.

targeting distinct biological processes (mechanisms of action). They fall into seven pharmacologic classes based on these unique mechanisms: Enbrel (tumor necrosis factor inhibitor), Januvia (dipeptidyl peptidase-4 inhibitor), Farxiga and Jardiance (sodium-glucose cotransporter-2 inhibitors), Eliquis and Xarelto (direct factor Xa inhibitors), Stelara (interleukin-12 and interleukin-23 inhibitors), Imbruvica (Bruton's tyrosine kinase inhibitor), and Entresto (angiotensin II receptor blocker and neprilysin inhibitor). Table 9 presents a comprehensive overview of the ten drugs: Eliquis, Enbrel, Entresto, Farxiga, Imbruvica, Januvia, Jardiance, NovoLog, Stelara, and Xarelto.

The distinction between regulatory pathways underscores the different approval processes involved for new drug applications (NDAs) and biologics license applications (BLAs). Small-molecule drugs, typically synthetic or semi-synthetic compounds with well-defined chemical structures, undergo a different evaluation process under NDAs, where regulators focus on the drug's chemical structure, manufacturing process, and clinical trial data. In contrast, biologics are typically large-molecule drugs derived from living organisms. Given their complex chemical structures, biologics undergo a distinct approval process under BLA, where regulators focus on challenges associated with their unique characteristics and manufacturing complexities. Establishing a better understanding of the mechanism of action is crucial both for BLAs and NDAs, as it helps regulators assess the drug's potential benefits and risks, determine appropriate dosing, and identify potential drug interactions.

As indicated in Table 9, these drugs have had an average market presence of 14.75 years, with biological products (products approved by regulators as BLA) holding the longest tenure, averaging 18 years from their initial regulatory approval by the FDA. The average age of initial patents granted on these drugs is 22.8 years, while it is 30.6 years for the three BLAs.

The collaborative nature of drug innovation is evident in the information on the original patentees and licensees of the drugs listed in Table 9. Only three drugs were exclusively developed and commercialized by the manufacturer: NovoLog/Fiasp by Novo Nordisk, Januvia by Merck, and Entresto by Novartis, the successor of Ciba-Geigy. Half of the drugs originated from companies italicized in the patentee/licensee column, which have been acquired by large biopharma companies and no longer operate independently. Changing ownership of these products over time due to mergers and acquisitions means that, for five drugs listed in Table 9, multiple parties have shared development costs and marketing rights.

From the list of patentees and licensees presented in Table 9, six companies stand out as biotech pioneers, ushering in the era of molecular biology. Centocor (founded in 1979), Amgen (1980), Immunex (1981), and Medarex (1987) were trailblazers in commercializing technologies that emerged from publicly funded research conducted at universities in the United States. Additionally, collaborations between government agencies and business corporations, exemplified by the Human Genome Project, played a pivotal role in the emergence of the first generation of genomics startups, including Celera Genomics, established in 1998.

The advent of targeted therapies has revolutionized the treatment landscape for various diseases, including the ten MFP drugs from four therapeutic classes – anticoagulants, antidiabetics/cardiovasculars, disease-modifying antirheumatics (DMARDs), and anticancer agents (see Table 9). To combat these diseases, scientists strive to gain a deeper understanding of the biological pathways involved, as shown in Table 10.

By meticulously focusing on specific molecular targets as outlined in Table 10, scientists have successfully developed therapies that surpass existing alternatives in terms of efficacy and adverse side effects. As a result of CCL within the broader research ecosystem, the scientific advancements and technological developments shown in Table 10 have enabled scientists to unravel the molecular mechanisms underlying diseases and identify potential targets for therapeutic interventions. This knowledge guides the design of effective drug therapies, making research into biological pathways a cornerstone of TDD.

To facilitate CMS' grasp of the complexities inherent in developing drugs subject to negotiations, we present a concise overview of the CCL processes that paved the way for the target-based drug discovery revolution, dramatically improving the productivity of drug R&D over the past two decades. In elucidating the CCL process which yielded drugs that targeted seven identified mechanisms of action shown in Table 10, we document the scientific and technological advancements that have deepened our understanding of disease mechanisms of action and targeted pathways, ultimately contributing to the development of the ten MFP drugs.

A. Antidiabetics and Cardiovascular Drugs

In the intricate network of biological pathways that orchestrate numerous processes within the body, disruptions often lead to the development of diseases such as diabetes. To combat these diseases, scientists strive to gain a deeper understanding of the biological pathways involved. By unraveling the molecular mechanisms underlying these disorders, potential targets for intervention can be revealed. This knowledge guides the design of effective drug therapies, making research into biological pathways a cornerstone of the *target-based* drug discovery approach.

In the absence of detailed knowledge of the biological processes underlying a disease, drug discovery historically relied on observing a desired change in the

Table 10 Scientific advancement and technological development in translational research that have enabled discovery of the ten MFP drugs

Mechanism of action	Targeted pathway(s)	Scientific advancement and technological development enabling discovery (time period)
Direct factor Xa inhibitors	Coagulation cascade	Structure-based drug design (1980s–ongoing), advances in medicinal chemistry (1970s–ongoing), unlocking Factor Xa's 3D structure (1990s–2000s)
Insulin analogs (rapid-acting)	Insulin signaling pathway	Recombinant DNA technology (1970s), protein engineering (1980s–ongoing), understanding of insulin structure–function relationships
DPP-4 inhibitors	Incretin pathway	Genomics/proteomics (1990s–ongoing), understanding of glucose regulation (1950s–ongoing), gut hormone research (1980s–ongoing), enzyme inhibitor design (1980s–ongoing)
SGLT2 inhibitors	Renal glucose reabsorption	Genomics/proteomics (1990s–ongoing), understanding of glucose regulation (1950s–ongoing), focus on kidney function (1960s–ongoing), metabolic–cardiorenal link (2000s–ongoing)
TNF inhibitors	Inflammatory response	Monoclonal antibody production (1970s–1980s), understanding of cytokines (1960s–ongoing), hybridoma technology (1975), humanization of antibodies (1980s–1990s)

Table 10 (cont.)

Mechanism of action	Targeted pathway(s)	Scientific advancement and technological development enabling discovery (time period)
NEP inhibitor/ARB	Renin-angiotensin-aldosterone system and natriuretic peptide system	Detailed knowledge of RAS (1970s–ongoing), combination therapy development (1990s–ongoing), finely tuning RAS (2000s–ongoing), drug combination science (1990s–ongoing)
IL-12/IL-23 inhibitors	Th1 and Th17 immune response pathways	Immunology advances (1950s–ongoing), cytokine profiling (1980s–ongoing), targeting upstream master regulators (1990s–ongoing), monoclonal antibody evolution (1980s–ongoing)

Sources: See Appendix I for Table 10 references

overall disease state or phenotype, a method known as phenotypic screening. A prime example is the discovery of the first diabetes therapies in the early twentieth century as researchers recognized that extracts from bovine or porcine pancreases could lower blood sugar levels in diabetic patients. This discovery led to the development of insulin products that revolutionized diabetes treatment, although at the time the exact molecular mechanisms of insulin action were not fully understood.

NovoLog/Fiasp: A Century of Innovation from Bovine to Modified Human Insulin and Insulin Asparts

In the early 1920s, researchers observed that removing the pancreas from dogs resulted in diabetes, which led to the discovery of insulin, a substance produced by the pancreas that regulates blood sugar levels (Bliss 2007). Scientists successfully isolated insulin from dog pancreases and showed that it could lower blood sugar levels in diabetic dogs. Companies like Novo Nordisk (then known as Nordisk Insulinlaboratorium, founded as a nonprofit foundation

Table 11 Development of fast-acting insulin analogs

Key scientific figures	rDNA technology pioneers
Initial discovery (timeframe)	Genentech (1980s), Novo Nordisk (1980s)
Drug brand (generic) name, year of FDA approval	**Novolog/NovoRapid (insulin aspart), 2000**
	Humalog (insulin lispro), 1996
	Apidra (insulin glulisine), 2004
	Fiasp (faster-acting insulin aspart), 2017
	Lyumjev (insulin lispro-aabc), 2020
	Admelog (insulin lispro-aabc), 2017
Manufacturer, 10-Year total sales (time period)	**Novo Nordisk, $48 billion (2014–23)**
	Eli Lilly, $30 billion (2014–23)
	Sanofi, $8 billion (2014–23)
	Novo Nordisk, $11.4 billion (2017–23)
	Eli Lilly, n/a
	Sanofi, n/a

Sources: Authors' analysis of S&P Compustat database and company 10-K reports. Also see Appendix I for other references used in Table 11.

in 1923 with the goal of helping people with diabetes) played a vital role in making insulin available for clinical use by developing methods to purify it from animal pancreases. Insulin manufacturers have since refined the purification and production processes of animal-derived insulin (Table 11).

In the 1970s and 1980s, the advent of molecular biology and protein engineering opened up new possibilities for insulin therapy (Li 2006; Rasmussen 2014). Enhanced understanding of insulin's molecular structure and its interaction with the insulin receptor enabled scientists to modify the structure of human insulin, creating analogs with altered pharmacokinetic properties. With the coming of recombinant DNA technology in the 1970s, Novo Nordisk transitioned to producing human insulin through genetic engineering (Novo Nordisk n.d.). This approach involves inserting the human insulin gene into bacteria or yeast, which then produces the hormone. This shift to recombinant human insulin was a major breakthrough, eliminating the risk of allergic reactions associated with animal-derived insulin and ensured a consistent supply of the hormone (Hughes 2011). This technological breakthrough led to the development of fast-acting insulin analogs like insulin aspart, marketed under the brand names Fiasp and NovoLog (Table 11).

The discovery of insulin aspart was a result of meticulous research that provided a deep understanding of insulin's structure–function relationships. By making specific modifications to the amino acid sequence of human insulin, scientists were able to create an analog that is absorbed more rapidly from the injection site and has a shorter duration of action compared to regular human insulin. This rapid onset and shorter duration make insulin aspart an ideal tool for managing post-meal blood glucose spikes, a critical aspect of diabetes management.

Fiasp, a newer formulation of insulin aspart, represents a further advancement in rapid-acting insulin therapy. It incorporates niacinamide, a vitamin B3 derivative, to accelerate the initial absorption of insulin aspart, resulting in an even faster onset of action. This advance allows for greater flexibility in mealtime insulin administration, potentially improving glycemic control and quality of life for patients.

Through CCL, gaining insight into insulin's structure–function relationships enabled scientists to create insulin analogs that offer significant advantages over traditional insulin preparations. For several decades these advances have impacted the landscape of diabetes management, providing patients with more effective and convenient treatment options. Companies developed different formulations with varying durations of action to better manage blood sugar levels while the biological pathways and mechanisms of action responsible for the misregulation of blood glucose levels in diabetic patients remain mostly unknown.

DPP-4 and SGLT2 Inhibitors Shift the Paradigm in Diabetes Treatment

While both phenotypic and target-based approaches have yielded effective diabetes treatments, they represent distinct strategies with different advantages and challenges. Phenotypic screening allows for drug discovery in the absence of detailed knowledge about disease mechanisms, but it can be more time-consuming and challenging to identify the specific molecular targets involved. Target-based drug discovery, on the other hand, is more precise and efficient but requires a thorough understanding of the underlying disease biology.

Many recent successors of insulin products in diabetes management owe their existence to the discovery of incretin hormones and their translation into drug therapies for major metabolic diseases such as diabetes and obesity. The discovery of glucagon-like peptides such as GLP-1 and GLP-2 in the 1980s marked a major breakthrough in diabetes research, providing a deeper understanding of glucose metabolism. This enhancement of understanding ultimately paved the way for new treatment options, most notably the recent blockbuster antidiabetic and weight loss medications Zepbound (tirzepatide) and Wegovy (semaglutide). These GLP-1 receptor agonists generated over $60 billion in sales in recent years for their developers: Eli Lilly and Novo Nordisk.

Januvia (Sitagliptin): The Market Leader in DPP-4 Inhibitors

Many novelty antidiabetics such as DPP-4 (dipeptidyl peptidase-4) and SGLT2 (sodium-glucose cotransporter-2) inhibitors are the result of target-based drug discovery (Table 12). Researchers identified DPP-4 and SGLT-2 as molecular targets based on new insights into diabetes pathology following the discovery of GLP-1, a gut hormone that plays a key role in glucose regulation by stimulating insulin secretion and suppressing glucagon release.

Enhanced understanding of glucose metabolism ultimately paved the way for researchers to develop new treatment options, including Januvia (sitagliptin), an inhibitor of *dipeptidyl peptidase 4* (DPP-4) enzyme that plays a critical role in glucose regulation. Enabling researchers to design drugs to inhibit these targets specifically and effectively lower blood sugar levels, Januvia exemplifies the extent to which target-based discovery is more efficient and precise than phenotypic screening as a drug discovery approach, as it directly addresses the underlying molecular causes of the disease (Cordes 2020).

The foundation for DPP-4 inhibitors was laid by decades of research in incretin hormones. While discovered initially in 1966, advances in genomics and proteomics in the 1990s allowed scientists to identify and characterize the DPP-4 enzyme as a molecular target that can play a crucial role in the breakdown of incretin hormones, which are responsible for stimulating insulin secretion and suppressing glucagon release (Ahrén 2019).

Building upon this knowledge, researchers began exploring the potential of DPP-4 inhibitors as a therapeutic approach for type 2 diabetes. The rationale was simple, yet elegant: by inhibiting DPP-4, these drugs could prolong the action of incretins, thereby enhancing the body's natural ability to regulate blood sugar levels (Cordes 2020).

Table 12 Development of DPP-4 inhibitors

Key scientific figures	D. Drucker, J. Habener
Initial discovery (timeframe)	U. of Toronto, HMS (1980s–1990s)
Drug brand (generic) name, year of FDA approval	**Januvia (sitagliptin), 2006**
	Onglyza (saxagliptin), 2009
	Tradjenta (linagliptin), 2011
	Nesina (alogliptin), 2013
Manufacturer, 10-year total sales (time period)	**Merck, $46.1B (2014–23)**
	AstraZeneca, $9.3B (2014–23)
	B. Ingelheim, $12.7B (2014–23)
	Takeda, $5.7B (2014–23)

Sources: Authors' own analysis from data in the S&P Compustat database and company 10-K reports. Also see Appendix I for other references used in Table 12.

The development of DPP-4 inhibitors also benefited from ongoing research in glucose regulation and gut hormone research, which spanned several decades. These studies provided a deeper understanding of the complex interplay between various hormones and enzymes involved in glucose metabolism, allowing scientists to identify specific targets for therapeutic intervention.

In the 1980s, advances in enzyme inhibitor design further accelerated the development of DPP-4 inhibitors. Researchers utilized techniques like virtual screening to identify small molecules that could effectively bind to and inhibit DPP-4. This led to the discovery of sitagliptin, which was subsequently developed into Januvia, the first DPP-4 inhibitor to receive regulatory approval.

Januvia, launched by Merck in 2006, quickly became a blockbuster drug, offering type 2 diabetes patients a new and effective treatment option. Its mechanism of action involves inhibiting DPP-4, thereby increasing the levels of active incretin hormones in the body. The results are increased insulin secretion, decreased glucagon secretion, and improved glycemic control.

The success of Januvia paved the way for the development of other DPP-4 inhibitors, like saxagliptin and linagliptin (Ahrén 2019). These drugs, while sharing a similar mechanism of action, have distinct chemical structures and pharmacokinetic properties, offering patients a range of options to suit their individual needs and significantly improving the lives of millions of people with type 2 diabetes.

Jardiance (Empagliflozin) and Farxiga (Dapagliflozin) Dominate the Market for SGLT2 Inhibitors

Further research into GLP-1's multifaceted actions shed light on the complex interplay of hormones and organs involved in glucose regulation, which indirectly prompted the exploration of other therapeutic targets, such as the sodium-glucose cotransporter 2 (SGLT2) in the kidneys. SGLT2 inhibitors work by blocking glucose reabsorption in the kidneys, leading to increased glucose excretion in urine and lower blood sugar levels.

Insights into the *renal glucose reabsorption pathway* in the early twentieth century enabled scientists to describe the role that the kidney plays in filtering and reabsorbing glucose from the blood. Performing a critical function within this pathway, scientists later developed an understanding of SGLT2, a transmembrane protein that is embedded in the cell membrane to act as a transporter and facilitate the movement of glucose molecules from the urine back into the bloodstream. Based on this new insight into mechanism of action, scientists were able to come up with the hypothesis that, through a drug intervention that inhibits SGLT2, it could be possible to boost glucose excretion (elimination) and lower the blood sugar levels in people with diabetes (Table 13).

Table 13 Development of SGLTs inhibitors

SGLT2 inhibitors	
Key scientific figures	E. Wright, B.A. Hirayama
Initial discovery (timeframe)	UCLA, UCSF (1970s–1990s)
Drug brand (generic) name, year of FDA approval	Invokana (canagliflozin), 2013–14 **Farxiga (dapagliflozin), 2014** **Jardiance (empagliflozin), 2014** Steglatro (ertugliflozin), 2017
Manufacturer, 10-year total sales (time period)	Janssen (J&J), $10.2B (2013-22) **AstraZeneca, $20.6B (2014-23)** **B. Ingelheim/Eli Lilly, $25.5B (2014-23)** Merck & Co, $1.7B (2017-23)

Source: Authors' own analysis from data in the S&P Compustat database and company 10-K reports. Also see Appendix I for other references used in Table 13.

The development of Farxiga (dapagliflozin) is a result of this *target-based* drug discovery approach, which involves identifying a specific molecular target (SGLT2) involved in a disease (diabetes) and then designing a drug that interacts with that target to modulate its function (inhibiting SGLT2 to prevent the kidneys from reabsorbing filtered glucose.)

The development and commercialization of SGLT2 inhibitors, such as Jardiance (empagliflozin) and Farxiga (dapagliflozin), represent an intriguing story of scientific innovation, corporate acquisitions, and strategic partnerships within the pharmaceutical industry. These drugs have not only transformed the treatment of type 2 diabetes but have also shown promise in managing cardiovascular and renal complications, highlighting their potential to revolutionize cardiometabolic medicine.

SGLT2 inhibitors work by inhibiting the SGLT2 protein in the kidneys, which is responsible for reabsorbing glucose into the bloodstream. By blocking this transporter, these drugs increase glucose excretion in the urine, effectively lowering blood sugar levels in patients with type 2 diabetes. This novel mechanism of action not only addresses hyperglycemia but also has additional benefits in managing cardiovascular and renal complications associated with diabetes.

The scientific foundation for SGLT2 inhibitors was laid by decades of research. A growing understanding of renal glucose reabsorption, starting in the 1950s, led to the identification of SGLT2 as a key player in this process. Advancements in genomics and proteomics in the 1990s further elucidated the structure and function of SGLT2, paving the way for the design of specific inhibitors. In addition, advances in medicinal chemistry and structure-based drug design enabled the creation of molecules that could effectively bind to and block SGLT2.

The development of SGLT2 inhibitors was also driven by a growing appreciation of the interconnectedness of metabolic, cardiovascular, and renal systems. The emerging concept of the metabolic–cardiorenal link in the 2000s highlighted the potential of SGLT2 inhibitors to not only improve glycemic control but also address cardiovascular and renal complications associated with diabetes. This insight led to extensive research and clinical trials that ultimately confirmed the multifaceted benefits of these drugs.

Amylin Pharmaceuticals, a company founded in 1987 to focus on metabolic disorders, played a pivotal role in the early development of SGLT2 inhibitors. The company's research efforts were driven by a deep understanding of glucose regulation and the potential of targeting renal glucose reabsorption as a novel therapeutic approach. Through a combination of scientific expertise, innovative research, and strategic collaborations, Amylin successfully developed dapagliflozin, which later became Farxiga.

Amylin faced financial challenges, however, and was eventually acquired by Bristol Myers Squibb (BMS) in 2012. Recognizing the potential of dapagliflozin, BMS further developed and commercialized the drug in collaboration with AstraZeneca. This strategic partnership leveraged the strengths of both companies, combining BMS's expertise in drug development and commercialization with AstraZeneca's global reach and experience in cardiovascular medicine.

Jardiance, another SGLT2 inhibitor, followed a similar trajectory. Boehringer Ingelheim (BI) is a German pharmaceutical company with a strong track record in respiratory and cardiovascular medicine. BI's success in developing empagliflozin stems from long-standing expertise in metabolic research and its commitment to innovative drug development. However, BI lacked the global infrastructure and commercialization expertise needed to bring Jardiance to a wider market.

While both Amylin and BI received some government funding for their research, the development of SGLT2 inhibitors was primarily driven by business investment and corporate expertise. The success of these drugs highlights the importance of scientific collaboration, strategic partnerships, and a deep understanding of the underlying biological mechanisms.

Entresto: A Heartfelt Journey of an Angiotensin II Receptor Blocker (Valsartan) That Meets Its Soulmate, Neprilysin Inhibitor (Sacubitril)

The development of Entresto (sacubitril/valsartan), a revolutionary medication for heart failure, is a prime example of the transformative power of target-based drug discovery and the iterative process of learning about biological pathways and mechanisms of action. This combination therapy, which targets two distinct pathways involved in heart failure, represents a departure from the traditional phenotypic screening approach that previously dominated drug development. By understanding the underlying molecular mechanisms of heart failure, scientists were able to design a drug that not only treats symptoms but also modifies the disease's progression.

Entresto is a combination drug with a neprilysin inhibitor (NEPi) and an angiotensin II receptor blocker that helps manage heart failure by relaxing blood vessels and promoting fluid excretion while maintaining stable blood pressure. The combination of a NEPi with an angiotensin II receptor blocker (ARB), as seen in Entresto, represents a paradigm shift in heart failure treatment. This combination therapy not only blocks the harmful effects of angiotensin II but also enhances the beneficial effects of natriuretic peptides, resulting in improved cardiac function and reduced mortality.

The evolution of treatments for cardiovascular diseases, particularly heart failure, is a story of scientific curiosity, incremental innovation, and the integration of diverse therapeutic approaches. This narrative is exemplified by the development of ARBs, NEPis, and their ultimate combination in the groundbreaking drug, Entresto.

The journey began with the elucidation of the renin-angiotensin-aldosterone system (RAAS), a complex hormonal cascade that plays a crucial role in blood pressure regulation and fluid balance. In the 1970s, researchers, including those at the precursor companies to Novartis (Ciba-Geigy and Sandoz), began to unravel the complexities of this system and discovered the role of angiotensin II in hypertension and heart failure. This groundbreaking research, which laid the groundwork for the development of ARBs, was often supported by government funding and academic collaborations.

The development of ARBs was made possible by advancements in medicinal chemistry and receptor pharmacology, with Novartis's predecessors playing a significant role in this research. Scientists were able to design molecules that specifically target and block the angiotensin II receptor, leading to the creation of drugs like losartan, valsartan, and irbesartan. Notably, virtual screening, a computational technique that allows for the rapid evaluation of vast chemical libraries, played a crucial role in identifying potential ARB candidates. Novartis's legacy companies, Ciba-Geigy and Sandoz, had a long history of research in this area, spanning several decades. Corporate research received significant support from government grants and academic collaborations.

ARBs quickly became a cornerstone in managing hypertension and heart failure, offering patients a well-tolerated and effective treatment option. Despite their success, however, researchers continued to explore new avenues to improve cardiovascular outcomes. This research led to the discovery of neprilysin, a neutral endopeptidase enzyme that degrades natriuretic peptides, hormones that promote vasodilation, diuresis, and natriuresis.

The research on neprilysin and its inhibitors was also a collaborative effort, involving both academic institutions and pharmaceutical companies. Government funding played a crucial role in supporting this research, enabling scientists to delve into the complex mechanisms of cardiovascular regulation and identify new therapeutic targets. Recognizing the potential of inhibiting neprilysin to enhance the beneficial effects of natriuretic peptides, scientists developed NEPis such as sacubitril.

The development of Entresto was a culmination of decades of research and development, building upon the knowledge gained from previous studies on the RAAS and the potential of combination therapies. The development of ARBs and NEPis, which ultimately contributed to the development of Entresto, is a testament to the power of scientific collaboration, the importance of government funding for foundational research, and the relentless pursuit of better treatments for cardiovascular diseases. These drugs, born from a deep understanding of the RAAS and the intricate interplay of various biological pathways, have transformed the landscape of heart failure management, offering hope and improved quality of life to millions of patients worldwide.

B. TNF and IL-12/IL-23 Inhibitors: The Transformation of Autoimmune Therapies with the Rise of DMARDs

Disease-modifying antirheumatic drugs (DMARDs) have revolutionized the treatment of autoimmune diseases, offering patients relief from debilitating symptoms and improved quality of life. Among the most notable DMARDs are tumor necrosis factor (TNF) inhibitors and interleukin-12/23 (IL-12/23) inhibitors, which have transformed the therapeutic landscape for conditions like rheumatoid arthritis, psoriasis, and Crohn's disease.

The cases of Enbrel (etanercept) and Stelara (ustekinumab), the only monoclonal antibodies in the Medicare price negotiations, are early success stories of the rDNA revolution. These two DMARDs target specific immune system components. They illustrate the critical importance of the target-based drug discovery approach, based on enhanced knowledge of biological processes involved in immune-system diseases such as rheumatoid arthritis (RA). This approach relies on a deep understanding of biological pathways and mechanisms of action, gleaned through decades of scientific advancements.

New insights into TNF signaling pathways, cytokine TNF, and its receptors (TNFR1 and TNFR2) resulted in the discovery of Enbrel (etanercept). Identifying TNF as a key driver of inflammation in RA made possible the development of this TNF inhibitor. Scientists realized that by targeting and blocking TNF, they could disrupt the inflammatory cascade and alleviate RA symptoms.

Similarly, the discovery of interleukins 12 and 23 (IL-12/23) as central players in the pathogenesis of psoriasis and other autoimmune diseases led to the development of Stelara. By targeting these cytokines, scientists could effectively reduce inflammation and improve outcomes for patients with these conditions.

These breakthroughs highlight the importance of understanding the underlying biological mechanisms of diseases. Through years of research and scientific inquiry, scientists have gained valuable insights into the intricate pathways that drive inflammation and immune responses. This knowledge has enabled the development of targeted therapies like Enbrel and Stelara, which offer more precise and effective treatment options for patients with debilitating autoimmune diseases.

Cytokines as an Early Success Story of the TDD Revolution

Ledley and colleagues estimate a low average of 20-year lag between the first description of the tyrosine kinase activity of retroviral oncogenes in the 1970s and approval of the first tyrosine kinase inhibitor (Beierlein et al. 2017). There was a similar lag between the discovery of TNF in 1975 and approval of the first TNF inhibitors. The journey involved in the discovery and development of Enbrel (etanercept), a large-molecule drug designed to block the action of a protein called TNF inhibitor, provides an excellent illustration of why the target-based drug discovery approach is inherently dependent on a deep understanding of disease mechanisms and molecular targets, developed through CCLs in which scientists in government agencies, business corporations, civil-society organizations, and academic institutions participated in the life-sciences knowledge ecosystem.

As discussed previously, AstraZeneca's transition from phenotypic drug discovery (PDD) to target-based drug discovery (TDD) in the early 2000s was a significant strategic shift, reflecting a broader industry trend toward more rational (target-based) drug design. This decision was likely influenced by CEO Pascal Soriot's previous research experience at Roche from 2006 to 2012, including a stint as CEO of Roche's US-based subsidiary, Genentech. Roche had established itself as a leader in drug innovation, particularly in high-risk, high-reward areas like cancer and immunotherapy. This success can be partially attributed to their early investment in fundamental biological research, exemplified by the establishment of the Roche Institute of Molecular Biology (RIMB) in 1964. This knowledge base allowed Roche to tap into the CCL within the US biopharma ecosystem, leveraging a growing body of knowledge in biology to translate discoveries into new drug therapies (Tulum 2018).

RIMB exemplifies CCL challenges in biopharma. It took Roche nearly three decades to integrate the knowledge and skills acquired through RIMB, permitting the company to expand its innovation capacity beyond traditional pharmaceuticals into the development of complex biologics. Confronting these challenges, RIMB played a pivotal role in the early years of the molecular biology revolution. It served as a magnet for top scientific talent at a time when the pharmaceutical industry struggled to attract academics into industrial research.

RIMB fostered a unique collaborative environment that fueled groundbreaking discoveries in molecular biology and biotechnology. As a leading research hub, it facilitated the exchange of ideas and nurtured collaborations among a close-knit group of scientists. In the 1970s, RIMB earned a reputation as a premier destination for postdoctoral researchers, rivaling academic institutions in its commitment to basic and applied research. It invited prominent scientists, including Herbert Boyer, co-founder of Genentech, to share their expertise with the burgeoning molecular biology community. Roche fostered a relationship with Boyer that ultimately led to the acquisition of Genentech, with Roche later transforming the US-based company into its global biotechnology R&D headquarters.

Sidney Pestka, the "father of interferon," joined RIMB in 1969 after a distinguished career that included groundbreaking research at the NIH's National Heart Institute and National Cancer Institute (Bürgi and Strasser 2009). At the Heart Institute, Pestka, mentored by Nobel laureate Marshall Nirenberg, made significant discoveries on how the genetic code of mRNA is translated into protein. His later research at the Cancer Institute sparked his interest in interferons, a class of proteins with antiviral properties, leading him to RIMB, where his pioneering work on interferon-based therapies revolutionized the treatment of various diseases, including cancer and hepatitis.

Under Pestka's leadership, RIMB significantly affected the development of both Enbrel and Stelara. Pestka's pioneering research on interferons, a type of cytokine, paved the way for Roferon-A, the first recombinant interferon approved for clinical use (Zoon 2017). This milestone not only advanced biotechnology but also laid the groundwork for future cytokine-based therapies.

Roche's contribution to cytokine research extended beyond RIMB, as the company held the patents for the fusion protein etanercept, the active ingredient in Enbrel. Immunex licensed these patents from Roche and developed Enbrel as a groundbreaking treatment for autoimmune diseases. Additionally, RIMB fostered a collaborative environment that spurred innovation (Weissbach and Fisher 2016). Menachem Rubinstein, a scientist at RIMB, partnered with Pestka to purify and characterize human leukocyte interferon, a crucial step in Roferon-A's development (Weizmann Institute 2007). Later, Rubinstein's protein fractionation method, refined at RIMB, played a pivotal role in understanding cytokine biology, ultimately contributing to the development of Enbrel (Weinreb 2013).

The RIMB's impact extended beyond immediate research. David H. Smith, a former RIMB scientist, co-founded Medarex, a pioneering biotechnology company that focused on antibody-based therapeutics. Smith's experience at RIMB, where he delved into monoclonal antibody research, laid the foundation for Medarex's success in this burgeoning field. Medarex, in partnership with Centocor (later acquired by Johnson & Johnson), played a pivotal role in the development of Stelara (ustekinumab). This innovative biologic drug, targeting IL-12 and IL-23, has become a cornerstone in the treatment of various inflammatory conditions, including psoriasis, psoriatic arthritis, Crohn's disease, and ulcerative colitis.

Thus, RIMB's legacy, along with Roche's patent ownership and subsequent licensing agreement with Immunex, indirectly influenced the development of two game-changing drugs, Enbrel and Stelara, through the work of its scientists and the knowledge generated within its collaborative research environment. The scientific expertise inherited from RIMB enabled Roche to contribute to the creation of these transformative medicines, underscoring the institute's far-reaching impact on the development of novel therapies.

Enbrel (Etanercept): A TNF Inhibitor That Emerged as a Breakthrough in Immunology

Etanercept, a TNF inhibitor, is a drug that works by specifically targeting the TNF signaling pathway (Table 14). It binds to and neutralizes TNF, thereby reducing inflammation and alleviating RA symptoms. This targeted approach demonstrates how understanding biological pathways can lead to the development of effective therapies for specific diseases.

The initial discovery of TNF dates back to the late nineteenth century when researchers observed tumor regression in cancer patients after bacterial infections (Graeber 2018, c. 2). This research led to the identification of a substance produced by immune cells that could kill tumor cells, initially named "tumor necrosis factor." It was not until the 1970s and 1980s, however, that the role of TNF in inflammation and autoimmune diseases began to be elucidated (Zarros et al. 2016).

Table 14 Development of TNF inhibitors

	TNF inhibitors
Key scientific figures	B. Beutler, D. Wallach
Initial discovery (timeframe)	Weizmann Institute (1980s–1990s)
	Immunex Corporation (1990s)
Drug brand (generic) name, year of FDA approval	**Enbrel (etanercept), 1998**
	Remicade (infliximab), 1998
	Humira (adalimumab), 2002
	Cimzia (certolizumab pegol), 2008
	Simponi (golimumab), 2009
Manufacturer, 10-year total sales (time period)	**Amgen, $66.6B (2014–23)**
	AbbVie, $192.5B (2014–23)
	J&J, $40.2B (2014–23)
	J&J, $24.6B (2014–23)
	UCB, $16.7B (2014–23)

Sources: See Appendix I for Table 14 references

Scientists discovered that TNF, a cytokine produced primarily by macrophages, played a central role in the inflammatory response, an insight that led to the exploration of TNF as a potential therapeutic target for inflammatory diseases such RA. In RA, the immune system mistakenly attacks the joints, causing chronic inflammation, pain, and damage. Researchers found that TNF levels were elevated in the joints of RA patients, suggesting its involvement in the disease process. This discovery spurred the development of TNF inhibitors, a class of drugs designed to block the action of TNF and reduce inflammation.

The FDA approved the first TNF inhibitors in 1998: infliximab (Remicade) in August followed by etanercept (Enbrel) in November. The approval of adalimumab (Humira), the world's all-time top-selling drug, came in 2002. These drugs revolutionized the treatment of RA, providing significant relief for patients who previously had limited treatment options. The success of TNF inhibitors demonstrated the power of targeting specific biological pathways to treat complex diseases, making possible further research and development in this field.

The story of Enbrel is marked by scientific innovation, corporate acquisitions, and legal battles. Initially patented in 1995, Immunex, a biotechnology company later acquired by Amgen, developed Enbrel. The drug's unique mechanism of action, involving a fusion protein that binds to TNF and inhibits its inflammatory activity, made it a game changer in the treatment of RA.

However, Enbrel's patent life has been the subject of ongoing legal disputes, with challenges from biosimilar manufacturers seeking to enter the market.

Stelara (Ustekinumab): An IL-12/IL-23 Inhibitors Targeting Upstream Regulators

In the 1990s, scientists identified interleukin-12 (IL-12) and IL-23 as key cytokines involved in the pathogenesis of psoriasis and other inflammatory diseases. This discovery spurred the development of IL-12/23 inhibitors, a class of drugs that target these cytokines upstream in the inflammatory cascade. Advances in biotechnology, particularly in monoclonal antibody evolution, enabled the creation of drugs like ustekinumab (Stelara), which has revolutionized the treatment of psoriasis and psoriatic arthritis (Table 15).

The development of Stelara involved a collaboration between Medarex, Centocor, and Johnson & Johnson. Medarex, known for its expertise in antibody engineering, developed the initial antibody, while Centocor, a subsidiary of Johnson & Johnson, conducted clinical trials and obtained regulatory approval. Stelara's unique mechanism of action, targeting both IL-12 and IL-23, has proven to be highly effective in managing psoriasis and its associated joint inflammation.

Aside from human insulin, these two DMARDs, Stelara and Enbrel, are the only biologic medicinal products included in the first round of Medicare price negotiations. The cost of these two large-molecule drugs to Medicare was $5.4 billion in 2022–2023. Stelara cost Medicare $120,000 per Medicare Part D program user, while Enbrel cost over $58,000 per user. Despite their medical benefits, the high cost of these therapies, coupled with complex patent claims and ongoing legal battles, underscores the challenges of ensuring affordable access to innovative medicines.

Table 15 Development of IL-12/IL-23 inhibitors

IL–12/IL–23 inhibitors	
Key scientific figures	G. Trinchieri, S. Gaffen
Initial discovery (timeframe)	NCI, U. of Pittsburgh (1990s–2000s)
Drug brand (generic) name, year of FDA approval	**Stelara (ustekinumab), 2009**
	Tremfya (guselkumab), 2017
	Ilumya (tildrakizumab), 2018
	Skyrizi (risankizumab), 2019
Manufacturer, 10-year total sales (time period)	**J&J, $59.9B (2014–23)**
	J&J, $12.6B (2017–23)
	Sun/Merck, $2.4B (2018–23)
	AbbVie, $7.1B (2019–23)

Source: See Appendix I for Table 15 references

C. Direct Factor Xa Inhibitors: A Revolution in Anticoagulant Therapy

Blood clots claim more lives annually than AIDS, breast cancer, and motor vehicle accidents combined. To combat this social loss, anticoagulants, often called blood thinners, have been developed. Among the most recent advancements in this field are direct factor Xa (FXa) inhibitors, a new generation of anticoagulants that have revolutionized treatment and prevention of thrombotic events. Eliquis (apixaban) and Xarelto (rivaroxaban) are two prominent examples of these drugs, each with unique development stories.

The discovery and development of direct FXa inhibitors were made possible by significant advancements in structure-based drug design, medicinal chemistry, and the ability to unlock the 3D structure of Factor Xa. Research since the 1980s has provided scientists with critical insights into the coagulation cascade and the central role of FXa in thrombin generation (Table 16).

Utilizing techniques like X-ray crystallography and computer modeling, researchers have been able to design small-molecule inhibitors that selectively bind and block FXa, effectively preventing clot formation. This targeted approach represents a significant advancement over traditional anticoagulants, such as warfarin, which often require close monitoring and dose adjustments due to their non-specific mechanism of action.

Eliquis (Apixaban): A Blockbuster Drug with a Complex History

Among the ten MFP drugs, Eliquis stands out as the costliest. From June 2022 to May 2023, it accounted for nearly one-third ($16.5 billion out of $50.5 billion) of Medicare's total expenditure on these ten products.

The complex history of Eliquis, involving the evolution of scientific understanding as well as mergers and acquisitions, highlights the intricate nature of drug

Table 16 Development of direct factor Xa inhibitors

	Direct factor Xa inhibitors
Key scientific figures	R. Scarborough
Initial discovery (timeframe)	Millennium Pharma. (1990s–2000s)
Drug brand (generic) name, year of FDA approval	**Xarelto (rivaroxaban), 2008** **Eliquis (apixaban), 2012** Savaysa (edoxaban), 2015 Bevyxxa (betrixaban), 2017
Manufacturer, 10-year total sales (time period)	**Bayer/J&J, $41.9B (2014-23)** **BMS/Pfizer, $52.1B (2012-21)** Daiichi Sankyo, $7.3B (2015-23) Portola, $0.4B (2017-23)

Sources: See Appendix I for Table 16 references

development and the challenges of balancing innovation with affordability. Eliquis, jointly developed and commercialized by BMS and Pfizer, quickly rose to prominence as a leading anticoagulant. In 2022 alone, it generated an enormous $11.8 billion in global sales for BMS, accounting for 26 percent of the company's total revenues. The drug's success can be attributed to its effectiveness in preventing strokes and systemic embolism in patients with nonvalvular atrial fibrillation, and its favorable safety profile compared to older anticoagulants.

Apixaban was discovered by scientists who joined BMS after it acquired DuPont Pharmaceuticals in 2001. DuPont had a long history in agricultural and veterinary pharmaceuticals and had serendipitously discovered the human use of warfarin, a widely prescribed anticoagulant originally developed as a rat poison.

Interestingly, the collaboration between BMS and Pfizer to develop and market apixaban was, in part, motivated by potential drug interactions between warfarin and Celebrex, a Pfizer drug for RA. This case highlights the interconnectedness of drug development and strategic considerations of pharmaceutical companies in bringing new products to market.

Xarelto (Rivaroxaban): A Collaborative Effort in the Pursuit of Safer Anticoagulation

Xarelto, also known by its generic name rivaroxaban, is a direct factor Xa (FXa) inhibitor that has become a cornerstone in treating and preventing thrombotic events. Developed by Bayer, a company with a rich history in agricultural and veterinary pharmaceuticals, Xarelto emerged from a concerted effort to create a new generation of oral anticoagulants with improved safety and efficacy profiles compared to traditional therapies.

The discovery of rivaroxaban by Bayer scientists was the culmination of extensive research and development in the field of coagulation. Recognizing the limitations of existing anticoagulants, such as warfarin, which required frequent monitoring and dose adjustments, Bayer embarked on a quest for a more convenient and predictable alternative. This strategy led to the exploration of direct FXa inhibitors, a class of drugs that specifically targets and inhibits FXa, a key enzyme in the coagulation cascade.

To navigate the complex regulatory landscape and commercialize Xarelto effectively, Bayer formed a strategic collaboration with Johnson & Johnson (J&J). This partnership leveraged Bayer's expertise in drug development and J&J's extensive distribution network and marketing capabilities. By joining forces, the two companies were able to accelerate the clinical development, regulatory approval, and market adoption of Xarelto.

The collaboration proved to be successful, with Xarelto gaining FDA approval in 2011 for the prevention of deep vein thrombosis (DVT) and pulmonary embolism (PE) in patients undergoing knee or hip replacement surgery. It has since been approved for various other indications, including stroke prevention in patients with nonvalvular atrial fibrillation and the treatment of DVT and PE.

From June 2022 to May 2023, Xarelto was prescribed to 1.4 million Medicare Part D enrollees, costing the program $6 billion. The development of Xarelto exemplifies the complex interplay of scientific innovation, regulatory hurdles, and commercial considerations in the pharmaceutical industry. The collaboration between Bayer and Johnson & Johnson proved to be instrumental in bringing this lifesaving drug to market, highlighting the importance of strategic partnerships in drug development.

D. BTK Inhibitors and the Discovery of Imbruvica (Ibrutinib) as a Breakthrough in Cancer Treatment

The development of Bruton's tyrosine kinase (BTK) inhibitors, a class of drugs designed to inhibit the growth and survival of cancer cells, represents a major advancement in cancer treatment. Imbruvica (ibrutinib), a prominent member of this class, is a revolutionary therapy for various B-cell malignancies, demonstrating remarkable efficacy and improving the lives of countless patients (Table 17).

The story of BTK inhibitors begins with a deeper understanding of B-cell signaling pathways and the role of BTK in these processes. B-cells are a type of white blood cell that plays a crucial role in the immune system. In certain cancers, however, B-cells can become malignant and proliferate uncontrollably. Max Planck Institute scientist Michael Reth identified BTK, a key enzyme involved in B-cell receptor signaling, in the late 1980s and early 1990s as a potential therapeutic target for these B-cell malignancies.

Table 17 Development of BTK inhibitors

Key scientific figures	O. Bruton, O. Witte
Initial discovery (timeframe)	Walter Reed Army Medical Center, UCLA (1950s–1990s)
Drug brand (generic) name, year of FDA approval	**Imbruvica (ibrutinib), 2013** Calquence (acalabrutinib), 2017 Brukinsa (zanubrutinib), 2019
Manufacturer, 10-year total sales (period)	**AbbVie, $43.7B (2014–23)** AstraZeneca, $8.8B (2017–23) BeiGene, $2.1B (2019–23)

Sources: See Appendix I for Table 17 references

Advancements in kinase inhibitor design and high-throughput screening techniques in the early 2000s facilitated the discovery and development of BTK inhibitors. Scientists were able to design small molecules that could specifically bind to and inhibit BTK, thereby disrupting the signaling pathways essential for the survival and proliferation of cancer cells.

Imbruvica, originally licensed to Pharmacyclics by Celera Genomics in 2006, emerged as a promising candidate in preclinical and clinical studies. The drug's unique mechanism of action, involving irreversible inhibition of BTK, showed remarkable efficacy in targeting B-cell malignancies.

In 2011, Pharmacyclics entered into a collaboration agreement with Johnson & Johnson's Janssen division to further develop and commercialize Imbruvica. This partnership leveraged the expertise of both companies, combining Pharmacyclics' scientific knowledge with Janssen's global reach and experience in drug development. Notably, in the same year, Pharmacyclics also established a Cooperative Research and Development Agreement (CRADA) with the NIH, further demonstrating the collaborative nature of drug development.

Upon the successful completion of clinical trials, Imbruvica received FDA approval in 2013 for the treatment of mantle cell lymphoma, a rare and aggressive type of blood cancer. It has since been approved for various other B-cell malignancies, including chronic lymphocytic leukemia and Waldenström's macroglobulinemia.

The success of Imbruvica not only transformed the treatment landscape for these cancers but also spurred further research and development in the field of BTK inhibitors. Second-generation BTK inhibitors, such as acalabrutinib, have since been developed, offering additional treatment options for patients.

In conclusion, the development of BTK inhibitors, particularly Imbruvica, exemplifies the power of scientific collaboration, technological innovation, and strategic partnerships in the pharmaceutical industry. The discovery of BTK as a therapeutic target, coupled with advancements in drug design and clinical research, has led to the creation of a new class of drugs that offer hope and improved outcomes for patients with other malignancies.

5 The Knowledge Ecosystem of Drug Discovery and Development, and the Fair Price for a Drug

Our introduction to this Element cites US Senator Howard Metzenbaum, US Representative Henry Waxman, and consumer crusader Ralph Nader, who, in congressional hearings in 1983 and 1985, called out the major pharmaceutical companies for price gouging. Subsequently, Congress pinned its legislative hopes for lowering drug prices on competition from generics, when a drug went off patent. For various reasons, however, as we outline in the introduction, that approach has not worked. Indeed, over the decades, as we also show, the problem of high and rising drug prices has gotten worse in the United States.

An irony of the US regime of unregulated drug prices is that we, the people (taxpayers, employees, patients), grant pharmaceutical companies the intellectual-property rights that empower them to price gouge us. In this Element, we have shown theoretically why price gouging is possible. The company reaps economies of scale that lower unit cost as output expands while it sells to a market in which there is a high level of price inelasticity of demand. In engaging in drug-price negotiations, CMS and indeed analysts everywhere need to understand this business model (note that it is not the one that they would have in mind from studying conventional economics).[8]

Back in the early 1980s, lawmakers should have insisted that, if pharmaceutical companies wanted government-granted patent monopolies on drugs, the US government had the social obligation to regulate drug prices. As legitimacy for this stance, there existed government regulation of the prices charged on, for example, electricity, by utilities companies deemed to be "natural monopolies" (Quigley 2017). In setting prices for electricity, the regulatory agency seeks (when it is not corrupted by bribes or revolving doors) to set a price that trades off the desire for affordability for consumers with the need for the utility company to have sufficient profits to fund improvement in and expansion of the supply of the product. The difference with pharmaceutical drugs is that there is far more uncertainty than is the case of electricity generation concerning whether the augmented investments in R&D funded by a higher drug price will actually result in a product that is improved and more accessible.

Even if a pharmaceutical company exhibits a high-failure rate of drug R&D, the principle that justifies drug-price regulation is the same as for a utility. In the case of pharmaceuticals, there is a need for a perspective, which we have sought to provide in this Element, on firm-level investment in drug innovation as part of the last stage of the evolution of a CCL-driven knowledge ecosystem that includes foundational and translational as well as clinical research. The analysis that we have provided can inform assessments of how well the CMS has done in representing the public interest in the first round of negotiations over the prices of the ten MFP drugs covered in this Element. Our approach also highlights the type of understanding that, for the sake of achieving "fair" prices, regulators should possess concerning the evolution of knowledge creation for the specific drugs that will be negotiated in future MFP rounds.

---

[8] See Lazonick (2024).

As we stated at the outset, the notion that the government has a social obligation to engage in drug-price negotiations has been a long time coming. In the early 1980s, when public concern with rising drug prices erupted, Ronald Reagan had been elected US president on a platform of across-the-board deregulation of industry, a position that had already been embraced by many leading Democrats in the late 1970s under the Carter administration (Stein 2011). By *not* trying to make the case for drug-price regulation, Democrats such as Metzenbaum and Waxman implicitly accepted Big Pharma's argument that, even if existing drugs would be less affordable, the higher drug prices would provide the profits to fund investment in drug innovation that would create value for society.

It also happens that in the first half of the 1980s, the ideology that a company should be run to maximize shareholder value (MSV) arose, subsequently evolving to dominate the practice of corporate resource allocation in the United States. In November 1982, the SEC adopted "license to loot" Rule 10b-18 (Jacobson and Lazonick 2026), and from 1984, established US-based industrial corporations, including, as we have documented, Merck and Pfizer, began to do large-scale open-market repurchases in addition to the corporate cash that they were paying to shareholders as dividends. In 1988, Pfizer heralded the new era of MSV with the cover of its annual report declaring that the company was "Building shareholder value through innovation." In the *1988 Annual Report*, under the heading "Building Shareholder Value," Pfizer explained:

> Our strategy is to emphasize research and development in all our business segments. Our spending on R&D will top half a billion dollars in 1989. That's twice what we spent in 1984.... The goal of our strategy is innovation. Innovative products enable us to meet needs in superior ways, to face competition and to adapt to changing business environments. They also create earning power. At Pfizer, we believe innovation is the soundest way to build shareholder value. (Pfizer 1988, p. 5)

Pfizer recorded only $7 million in buybacks in 1988, but over the next decade, the company repurchased $5.6 billion, representing 40 percent of net income, on top of 44 percent of net income paid as dividends. And, as we have seen, Pfizer was just getting going in its distributions of corporate cash to shareholders. In 1999–2008, it spent $53.1 billion on buybacks (64 percent of net income), and in 2009–2018 $67.9 billion (57 percent), all the while paying out about 57 percent of profits as dividends.

To our knowledge, nobody in Congress – not even Henry Waxman – who was concerned about high drug prices took notice of the fact that, like so many other US-based companies, Pfizer's senior executives were allocating the company's profits, provided by those high prices, to prop up the company's stock price.[9] This "misallocation" of resources in the pharmaceutical industry did not garner attention until 2016, when the Academic-Industry Research Network submitted a comment, "Life Sciences? How 'Maximizing Shareholder Value' Increases Drug Prices, Restricts Access, and Stifles Innovation," to the United Nations Secretary-General's High-Level Panel on Access to Medicines (Lazonick et al. 2016).[10]

As we have argued in this Element, it is the adherence to shareholder-value ideology that permits senior pharmaceutical executives to assume that, in principle, all the value to society created by an innovative drug that their company sells should be captured in the price that the company charges for the drug *and* that all that value belongs to shareholders. As we have seen in the cases of Bourla at Pfizer and Frazier at Merck, pharmaceutical CEOs recognize that, even with unregulated prices, a variety of circumstances influence the price that they set on a drug so that the company cannot capture its full "value to society." The CEOs nevertheless assume that their company has the right to that value. Hence, in public posturing or (as is now the case) negotiations with Medicare, the pharmaceutical company will posit that, as a matter of principle, the "maximum fair price" to which its shareholders have a right should represent the drug's "value to society." From that lofty position, the pharmaceutical companies and their allies can represent any lower price on its product as a concession to society.

Regulators need to be able to confront this MSV position, arguing from the outset that, in setting a "fair" price, there are many other stakeholders, including workers, taxpayer, and patients, who have rights to capture significant portions of value to society. The decades of knowledge creation that enabled the development of the ten MFP drugs in the current negotiation underscore the complex interplay of government agencies, civil-society organizations, academic institutions, and business corporations in processes of scientific discovery and technological advancement in the pharmaceutical industry. In negotiating drug prices, CMS negotiators who have access to these types of case histories can address the critical issue of the limited value-added contribution of the pharmaceutical companies in question.

---

[9] Exceptionally, in the summer of 2008 four Congressional Democrats – Rep. Rahm Emanuel (D-IL), Rep. Edward Markey (D-MA), Sen. Robert Menendez (D-NJ), and Sen. Charles Schumer (D-NY) – took aim at stock repurchases by the big oil companies, after Exxon Mobil, by far the largest repurchaser of stock ($144 billion in 2000–2008), had announced record second quarter profits of $11.7 billion, of which $8.8 billion went to stock buybacks. In a letter to oil industry executives, the Congressmen asked them to "pledge to greatly increase the ratio of investments in production and alternatives to the amount of stock buybacks this year and next by investing much more of your profits into exploration and production on the leases you have been awarded in the U.S., and in the research and development of promising alternative energy sources." See US Congress (2008), and Hays and Ivanovich (2008).

[10] See also Lazonick et al. (2017).

The individual stories of these ten MFP drugs reveal the evolving landscape of the pharmaceutical industry, with increasing collaborations and mergers between companies, as seen in the development of Eliquis, Stelara, and Imbruvica. These partnerships often leverage the strengths of different organizations, combining scientific expertise with commercial capabilities to accelerate drug development and market access. These combinations, however, also raise questions about the potential for market concentration and its impact on drug prices.

Even when confronted with this information, the pharmaceutical companies could seek to defend the principle of value-based pricing by contending that, when purchasing inputs to the drug development process, the company whose drug price is being negotiated has paid for prices of those inputs based on the value to society that they create. It would then follow that, in terms of profits, the pharmaceutical company is only receiving its *value-added* to society.

A fundamental problem with that argument is that innumerable scientists and related personnel, going back decades, working in government agencies, civil-society organizations, academic institutions, and business corporations, have gone to work every day, receiving remuneration for the supply of their skills and efforts at prevailing salary levels that bear little, if any, relation to the value of their labor to society as measured by the value of the safe and effective medicines that ultimately become available to society. In doing their work, these hardworking people may very well be incentivized by the notion that their contributions will eventually create *value for society*. But they do not get paid according to a notion of "value to society," not only because that value of the safe and effective drugs is not known at the time that they are doing their work but also because they are individuals engaged in a vast process of collective and cumulative learning in foundational, translational, and clinical research.

Given the process of knowledge creation that goes into the discovery and development of a drug that makes it to market, there is no reason why the entity that sells it on the market should be the one that sets a price to capture value to society. In negotiating drug prices, regulators need only consider whether a higher MFP will, in fact, enable the pharmaceutical company to cover the cost of developing, manufacturing, and delivering the existing product while leaving sufficient profits (after paying reasonable dividends to shareholders) in the hands of the company to invest in the next round of innovative products. If the pharmaceutical company has plans to invest in novel therapies that can create great value for society, CMS might want to incentivize and reward this socially progressive behavior in the form of a higher MFP. Beyond that, however, the pharmaceutical company should get an MFP that, as is generally the case in a civilized society, incentivizes and rewards their personnel for doing their jobs.

References

Ahrén, Bo. "DPP-4 Inhibition and the Path to Clinical Proof." *Frontiers in Endocrinology* 10, 2019: 376.

Anonymous. "Stock Offering to Public Today; $5,940,000 Common of Pfizer & Co. to be Handled by Underwriting Group." *New York Times*, June 23, 1942.

Arthritis Foundation. "Rheumatoid Arthritis (RA)." Last modified October 15, 2021. Accessed August 14, 2024.

Ashley, Euan. "Towards Precision Medicine." *Nature Reviews Genetics* 17, 9, 2016: 507–522.

Bartfai, Tamas, and Graham Lees. *Drug Discovery: From Bedside to Wall Street*. Academic Press, 2006.

Beierlein, Jennifer, Laura McNamee, and Fred Ledley. "As Technologies for Nucleotide Therapeutics Mature, Products Emerge." *Molecular Therapy – Nucleic Acids* 9, 2017: 379–386.

Bliss, Michael. *The Discovery of Insulin*. University of Chicago Press, 2007.

Blundell, Tom. "Protein Crystallography and Drug Discovery: Recollections of Knowledge Exchange between Academia and Industry." *International Union of Crystallography Journal* 4, 4, 2017: 308–321.

Bourla, Albert. *Moonshot: Inside Pfizer's Nine-Month Race to Make the Impossible Possible*. Harper Business, 2022.

Bürgi, Michael, and Bruno Strasser. "Pharma in Transition: New Approaches to Drug Development at F. Hoffmann-La Roche & Co, 1960–1980." In *Perspectives on 20th-Century Pharmaceuticals*, edited by Viviane Quirke and Judy Slinn, Oxford University Press, 2009: 391–432.

Burns, Tobias, and Karl Evers-Hillstrom. "Democrats Add Stock Buyback Tax, Scrap Carried Interest to Win Sinema over." *The Hill*, August 2, 2022.

Bush, Vannevar, and Rush Holt. *Science, the Endless Frontier*. Princeton University Press, 2021.

Callaway, Ewen. "The Revolution Will Not Be Crystallized: A New Method Sweeps through Structural Biology." *Nature* 525, 7568, 2015: 172–174.

Collington, Rosie, and William Lazonick. *Pricing for Medicine Innovation: A Regulatory Approach to Support Drug Development and Patient Access*. *Institute for New Economic Thinking Working Paper*, January 28, 2022.

Collins, Francis. "Implications of the Human Genome Project for Medical Science." *JAMA* 285, 5, 2001: 540–544.

Congressional Budget Office (CBO). *How CBO Estimated the Budgetary Impact of Key Prescription Drug Provisions in the 2022 Reconciliation Act*, February 17, 2023. Accessed August 14, 2024.

Cook, David, Dearg Brown, Robert Alexander, et al. "Lessons Learned from the Fate of AstraZeneca's Drug Pipeline: A Five-Dimensional Framework." *Nature Reviews Drug Discovery* 13, 6, 2014: 419–431.

Cordes, Eugene. *Hallelujah Moments: Tales of Drug Discovery*. 2nd ed. Oxford University Press, 2020.

Cui, Miao, Chao Cheng, and Lanjing Zhang. "High-Throughput Proteomics: A Methodological Mini-Review." *Laboratory Investigation* 102, 11, 2022: 1170–1181.

Davis, Rob, Dean Li, Jennifer Zachary, and Jannie Oosthuizen. "The Inflation Reduction Act's Negative Impact on Patient-Focused Innovation, Value and Access." Open letter *from Merck senior executives to the Merck community*, June 6, 2022.

Feldman, Robin. "The Price Tag of 'Pay-for-Delay.'" *Science and Technology Law Review* 23, 1, 2022: 1–49.

Graeber, Charles. *The Breakthrough: Immunotherapy and the Race to Cure Cancer*. Twelve, 2018.

Hays, Kristen, and David Ivanovich. "Politicians Fume as Exxon Profits soar to U.S. Record." Houston Chronicle, August 1, 2008.

Hopkins, Matt, and William Lazonick. "The Mismeasure of Mammon: Uses and Abuses of Executive Pay Data." *Institute for New Economic Thinking* Working Paper, October 2016.

Hopkins, Matt, and William Lazonick. "Tesla as Global Competitor: Strategic Control in the EV Transition." *Institute for New Economic Thinking* Working Paper, September 2024.

Horwitz, Sari. "Drug Industry Accused of Gouging Public." *Washington Post*, July 15, 1985.

Hughes, Sally. *Genentech: The Beginnings of Biotech*. University of Chicago Press, 2011.

Ignatius, Adi. "'Businesses Exist to Deliver Value to Society' – A Conversation with Merck CEO Kenneth Frazier." Harvard Business Review, 96, 2, March–April 2018: 82–87.

Inglese, James, Ronald L. Johnson, Anton Simeonov, et al. "High-Throughput Screening Assays for the Identification of Chemical Probes." *Nature Chemical Biology* 3, 8, 2007: 466–479.

Jacobson, Ken, and William Lazonick. "A License to Loot: SEC Rule 10b-18 and Alternative Theories of Capital Formation." *The Academic-Industry Research Network Working Paper*, forthcoming 2026.

Kornberg, Arthur. *The Golden Helix: Inside Biotech Ventures*. University Science Books, 1995.

Lazonick, William. *Competitive Advantage on the Shop Floor*. Harvard University Press, 1990.

Lazonick, William. "Innovative Enterprise Solves the Agency Problem: The Theory of the Firm, Financial Flows, and Economic Performance." *Institute for New Economic Thinking, INET Working Paper*, August 28, 2017.

Lazonick, William. "The Functions of the Stock Market and the Fallacies of Shareholder Value." In *Corporate Governance in Contention*, edited by Ciaran Driver and Grahame Thompson, Oxford University Press, 2018: 117–151.

Lazonick, William. "The Theory of Innovative Enterprise: Foundations of Economic Analysis." In *The Oxford Handbook of the Corporation*, edited by Thomas Clarke, Justin O'Brien, and Charles O'Kelley. Oxford University Press, 2019: 489–514.

Lazonick, William. "Maximizing Shareholder Value as an Ideology of Predatory Value Extraction." In *The Emergence of Corporate Governance: People, Power, and Performance*, edited by Knut Sogner and Andrea Colli. Routledge Taylor & Francis Group, New York, 2021: 170–186.

Lazonick, William. "Corporate Governance for the Common Good: The Theory of Innovative Enterprise as a Guide to Progressive Policy Reform." *The Academic-Industry Research Network* AIR Report #23–09/16, September 16, 2023a.

Lazonick, William. *Investing in Innovation: Confronting Predatory Value Extraction in the U.S. Corporation*. Cambridge University Press, 2023b.

Lazonick, William. "Is the Most Unproductive Firm the Foundation of the Most Efficient Economy? Penrosian Learning Confronts the Neoclassical Fallacy." *International Review of Applied Economics* 38, 1–2, 2024: 58–89.

Lazonick, William, and Jang-Sup Shin. *Predatory Value Extraction: How the Looting of the Business Corporation Became the U.S. Norm and How Sustainable Prosperity Can Be Restored*. Oxford University Press, 2020.

Lazonick, William, and Matt Hopkins. "If the SEC Measured CEO Pay Packages Properly, They Would Look Even More Outrageous." *Harvard Business Review*, December 22, 2016.

Lazonick, William, and Matt Hopkins. "Comment on the Pay Ratio Disclosure Rule." U.S. Securities and Exchange Commission, March 21, 2017.

Lazonick, William, Mustafa Erdem Sakınç, and Matt Hopkins. "Why Stock Buybacks Are Dangerous for the Economy." *Harvard Business Review*, January 7, 2020.

Lazonick, William, and Öner Tulum. "US Biopharmaceutical Finance and the Sustainability of the Biotech Business Model." *Research Policy* 40, 9, 2011: 1170–1187.

Lazonick, William, and Öner Tulum. "Sick with 'Shareholder Value': US Pharma's Financialized Business Model during the Pandemic." *Competition & Change* 28, 2, 2024: 251–273.

Lazonick, William, Matt Hopkins, Ken Jacobson, Mustafa Erdem Sakinç, and Öner Tulum. *Life Sciences? How "Maximizing Shareholder Value" Increases Drug Prices, Restricts Access, and Stifles Innovation.* Submission to the United Nations Secretary-General's High-Level Panel on Access to Medicines, February 28, 2016.

Lazonick, William, Matt Hopkins, Ken Jacobson, Mustafa Erdem Sakinç, and Öner Tulum . "U.S. Pharma's Business Model: Why It Is Broken, and How It Can Be Fixed." In *The Routledge Handbook of the Political Economy of Science*, edited by David Tyfield, Rebecca Lave, Samuel Randalls, and Charles Thorpe. Routledge, London, 2017: 83–100.

Li, Jie. *Laughing Gas, Viagra, and Lipitor*, Oxford University Press, 2006.

Longo, Nicole. "By the Numbers: Patients Lose When the Government Sets Prices," PhRMA, July 8, 2022.

Malhotra, Vik, and Steve Van Kuiken. "Voices of CEO Excellence: Merck's Ken Frazier." McKinsey & Company, June 12, 2023.

Mann, Brian, and Martha Bebinger. "Purdue Pharma, Sacklers Reach $6 Billion Deal with State Attorneys General." *NPR*, March 3, 2022.

McElwee, Frederick, Amanda Cole, Louis P. Garrison Jr, and Adrian Towse. "Federal Support Should Not Be a Factor in Determining Pharmaceutical Prices under the IRA," *HealthAffairs*, June 14, 2024.

McNamee, Laura, and Fred Ledley. "Modeling Timelines for Translational Science in Cancer; the Impact of Technological Maturation." *PLOS ONE* 12, 3, 2017: e0174538.

Merck & Co. v. Xavier Becerra. *U.S. Secretary of Health & Human Services; and U.S. Department of Health & Human Services*, Civil Action No. *1:23-Cv-01615*, United States District Court of the District of Columbia, June 6, 2023.

Mikulic, Matej. "Market Share of the Leading Global Pharmaceutical Markets 2022." *Statista*. May 22, 2024.

Mohs, Richard, and Nigel Greig. "Drug Discovery and Development: Role of Basic Biological Research." *Alzheimer's & Dementia: Translational Research & Clinical Interventions* 3, 4, 2017: 651–657.

Morgan, Paul, Dean G. Brown, Simon Lennard, et al. "Impact of a Five-Dimensional Framework on R&D Productivity at AstraZeneca." *Nature Reviews Drug Discovery* 17, 3, 2018: 167–181.

Nar, Herbert. "The Role of Structural Information in the Discovery of Direct Thrombin and Factor Xa Inhibitors." *Trends in Pharmacological Sciences* 33, 5, 2012: 279–288.

Neill, Ushma. "A Conversation with Dan Drucker." *Journal of Clinical Investigation* 131, 18, 2021: e154150. https://doi.org/10.1172/JCI154150.

Novo Nordisk. "Insulin 100 Years." *Novo Nordisk*. n.d. Accessed August 10, 2024.

OECD. *Health at a Glance 2023: OECD Indicators*. Organisation for Economic Co-operation and Development, 2023.

Patients for Affordable Drugs. "Statement: Court rejects Claims by Novo Nordisk Lawsuit in Sixth Straight Legal Victory for Medicare Negotiation and Patients." Novo Nordisk Press Release, July 31, 2024.

Petsko, Gregory. "Dawn of Structural Biology." In *A Century of Nature: Twenty-One Discoveries That Changed Science and the World*, edited by Laura Garwin and Tim Lincoln, University of Chicago Press, 2003: 85–104.

Pfizer. *Annual Report*, 1988.

Pfizer. *Event Brief of Q4 2019 Pfizer Inc Earnings Call – Final*. CQ FD Disclosure, January 28, 2020.

Pfizer. "Pfizer Reports First-Quarter 2022 Results." Pfizer press release. May 3, 2022a.

Pfizer. "Pfizer's Second Quarter Sees Historic Sales and Bold Goals." Pfizer Investor Insights. July 28, 2022b.

Pharmaceutical Research and Manufacturers of America (PhRMA). "Middlemen: Over Half of Every Dollar Spent on Medicines Goes to Middlemen and Others." Accessed August 14, 2024a.

Pharmaceutical Research and Manufacturers of America (PhRMA). "Research and Development Policy Framework." Accessed August 14, 2024b.

Prakash, Snigdha, and Vikki Valentine. "Timeline: The Rise and Fall of Vioxx." *NPR*, November 10, 2007.

Quigley, Fran. *Prescription for the People: An Activist's Guide to Making Medicine Affordable for All*. Cornell University Press, 2017.

Rasmussen, Nicolas. *Gene Jockeys: Life Science and the Rise of Biotech Enterprise*. Johns Hopkins University Press, 2014.

Robinson, Mark. "Translational Medicine: Science, Risk and an Emergent Political Economy of Biomedical Innovation." In *The Routledge Handbook of the Political Economy of Science*, Edited by David Tyfield, Rebecca Lave, Samuel Randalls, and Charles Thorpe. Routledge, 2017: 249–262.

Roumie, Christianne. "The Doughnut Hole: It's About Medication Adherence." *Annals of Internal Medicine* 156, 11, 2012: 834–835.

Roy, Victor. *Capitalizing a Cure: How Finance Controls the Price and Value of Medicines*. University of California Press, 2023.

Sampat, Bhaven. "Mission-Oriented Biomedical Research at the NIH." *Research Policy* 41, 10, 2012: 1729–1741.

Sayers, Eric W., Jeffrey Beck, Evan E. Bolton, et al. "Database Resources of the National Center for Biotechnology Information." *Nucleic Acids Research* 50, 1, 2022: D20–D26.

Scannell, Jack W., Alex Blanckley, Helen Boldon, and Brian Warrington. "Diagnosing the Decline in Pharmaceutical R&D Efficiency." *Nature Reviews Drug Discovery* 11, 3, 2012: 191–200.

Siegel, Rebecca L., Kimberly D. Miller, Nikita Sandeep Wagle, and Ahmedin Jemal. "Cancer Statistics, 2023." *CA: A Cancer Journal for Clinicians* 73, 1, 2023: 17–48.

Singh, Vandana. "Pfizer CEO Fires back on US Drug Pricing Reforms: 'Negotiation with a Gun to Your Head.'" *Bezinga.com*, May 12, 2023.

Sismondo, Sergio. "Controlled Flows of Pharmaceutical Knowledge." In *The Routledge Handbook of the Political Economy of Science*. Edited by David Tyfield, Rebecca Lave, Samuel Randalls, and Charles Thorpe. Routledge, 2017: 119–131.

Span, Paula. "Medicare's Part D Doughnut Hole Has Closed! Mostly. Sorta." *New York Times*, January 17, 2020.

Stein, Judith. *Pivotal Decade: How the United States Traded Factories for Finance in the Seventies*. Yale University Press, 2011.

Stockwell, Brent. *The Quest for the Cure: The Science and Stories behind the Next Generation of Medicines*. Columbia University Press, 2011.

Stolberg, Sheryl, and Rebecca Robbins. "Drugmakers are 'throwing the kitchen sink' to halt Medicare price negotiations," *New York Times*, July 23, 2023.

The White House. "FACT SHEET: Biden-Harris Administration Announces New, Lower Prices for First Ten Drugs Selected for Medicare Price Negotiation to Lower Costs for Millions of Americans." White House Briefing Room. August 15, 2024.

Tulum, Öner. "Innovation and Financialization in the U.S. Biopharmaceutical Industry." Doctoral dissertation, University of Ljubljana, 2018.

Tulum, Öner, Ellen Chappelka, Ken Jacobson, and William Lazonick. "INET-AIR Covid Vaccine Project." The Academic-Industry Research Network, 2021–2022.

Tulum, Öner, Antonio Andreoni, and William Lazonick. *From Financialisation to Innovation in UK Big Pharma: AstraZeneca and GlaxoSmithKline*. Cambridge University Press, 2023.

Tulum, Öner, and William Lazonick. "Moderna; Science for Money." *The Academic-Industry Research Network Working Paper*, May 14, 2024.

Ubl, Stephen. "An Open Letter to Congress: Stand with Patients and Future Cures," PhRMA. August 4, 2022.

United for Medical Research. *NIH's Role in Sustaining the U.S. Economy.* UnitedforMedicalResearch.org, March 2024.

U.S. Centers for Disease Control (CDC). "Heart Disease Facts." Heart Disease. June 22, 2023a.

U.S. Centers for Disease Control (CDC). "National Diabetes Statistics Report." Diabetes. February 28, 2023b.

U.S. Centers for Disease Control (CDC). "Data and Statistics on Venous Thromboembolism." Venous Thromboembolism (Blood Clots). May 22, 2024.

U.S. Centers for Medicare and Medicaid Services (CMS). "Fact Sheet: Medicare Drug Price Negotiation Program: Selected Drugs for Initial Price Applicability Year 2026." August 2023.

U.S. Congress. *The Patent Term Restoration Act of 1983: Hearings Before the Subcommittee on Patents, Copyrights, and Trademarks of the Committee on the Judiciary, United States Senate, Ninety-Eighth Congress, First Session*, June 22, July 19 and August 2, 1983.

U.S. Congress. *Public Law 98–417: Drug Price Competition and Patent Term Restoration Act*, September 24, 1984.

U.S. Congress. "Democrats Tell Big Oil: Spend More on Production and Renewable Energy, Less on Stock Buybacks before Making Demands for New Drilling Leases." US Congressional Documents and Publications, July 31, 2008.

U.S. Department of Health and Human Services (HHS), Office of the Assistant Secretary for Planning and Evaluation. *Comparing Prescription Drugs in the U.S. and Other Countries: Prices and Availability.* ASPE Contractor Project Report, February 2024.

U.S. Department of Labor, Bureau of Labor Statistics (BLS). "All Items in U.S. City Average, All Urban Consumers, Not Seasonally Adjusted (CPI-All, CUUR0000SA0); Medical Care in U.S. City Average, All Urban Consumers, Seasonally Adjusted (CPI-MC, CUUR0000SAM); Prescription Drugs in U.S. City Average, All Urban Consumers, Not Seasonally Adjusted (CPI-Rx, CUUR0000SEMF01)." n.d. Accessed August 14, 2023.

U.S. Food and Drug Administration (FDA). "Search Orphan Drug Designations and Approvals." Accessed September 8, 2024.

U.S. National Human Genome Research Institute (NHGRI). "Biological Pathways Fact Sheet." Accessed August 18, 2024.

U.S. National Institutes of Health (NIH), Office of Budget. "Appropriations History by Institute/Center (1938 to Present)." Accessed August 14, 2024a.

U.S. National Institutes of Health (NIH). "Operating Plan for FY 2024." Accessed August 14, 2024b.

U.S. National Institutes of Health (NIH). "Supplementary Appropriation Data Table for History of Congressional Appropriations, Fiscal Years 2020–2023." Accessed August 14, 2024c.

U.S. Patent and Trademark Office (USPTO). "Patent Term Calculator." Accessed August 13, 2024.

Venkatraman, Srikanth. "Discovery of Boceprevir, a Direct-Acting NS3/4A Protease Inhibitor for Treatment of Chronic Hepatitis C Infections." *Trends in Pharmacological Sciences* 33, 5, 2012: 289–294.

Venker, Brett, Kevin Stephenson, and Walid Gellad. "Assessment of Spending in Medicare Part D If Medication Prices from the Department of Veterans Affairs Were Used." *JAMA Internal Medicine* 179, 3, 1, 2019: 431–433.

Walker, Darren. *From Generosity to Justice: A New Gospel of Wealth*. Disruption Books, 2023.

Watson, James D. "The Human Genome Project: Past, Present, and Future." *Science* 248, 4951, 1990: 44–49.

Weber, Jonathan. "Is Pfizer Stock a Buy after Strong Earnings? Massive Profits Won't Last." *Seeking Alpha*, August 4, 2022.

Weinreb, Gali. "The Israel Inspired Revolution in Arthritis Treatment." *Globes*, July 3, 2013.

Weissbach, Herbert, and David Fisher. *A Camelot of the Biomedical Sciences: The Story of the Roche Institute of Molecular Biology*. RIMB Adventures, 2016.

Weizmann Institute. "The Interferon Story – Life Sciences." Weizmann Wonder Wander - Life Sciences. May 6, 2007.

Zarros, Apostolos, Emma M. Jones, and Elizabeth M. Tansey, eds. "The Recent History of Tumour Necrosis Factor (TNF). In *Transcript of Wellcome Witness to Contemporary Medicine*, vol. 60. London: Queen Mary University of London, 2016.

Zerhouni, Elias. "Translational and Clinical Science – Time for a New Vision." *New England Journal of Medicine* 353, 15, 2005: 1621–1623.

Zheng, Heping, Katarzyna B. Handing, Matthew D. Zimmerman, et al. "X-Ray Crystallography over the Past Decade for Novel Drug Discovery – Where Are We Heading Next?" *Expert Opinion on Drug Discovery* 10, 9, 2015: 975–989.

Zheng, Wei, Xiaoqin Dai, Binyao Xu, Wei Tian, and Jianyou Shi. "Discovery and Development of Factor Xa Inhibitors (2015–2022)." *Frontiers in Pharmacology* 14, 2023: 1105880.

Zhou, Edward W., Paula G. Chaves da Silva, Debbie Quijada, and Fred Ledley. "Considering Returns on Federal Investment in the Negotiated 'Maximum Fair Price' of Drugs under the Inflation Reduction Act: An Analysis." *Institute for New Economic Thinking* Working Paper. February 2024.

Zoon, Kathryn. "Sidney Pestka (1936–2016)." *Journal of Interferon & Cytokine Research* 37, 2, 2017: 51–51.

References used in Tables 8–17

Table 8

PPD and first-generation anticoagulants:

Calado, Cecília. "Bridging the Gap between Target-Based and Phenotypic-Based Drug Discovery." *Expert Opinion on Drug Discovery* 19, 7, 2024: 789–798.

Heestermans, Marco, Géraldine Poenou, Hind Hamzeh-Cognasse, Fabrice Cognasse, and Laurent Bertoletti. "Anticoagulants: A Short History, Their Mechanism of Action, Pharmacology, and Indications." *Cells* 11, 20, 2022: 3214. https://doi.org/10.3390/cells11203214.

Li, *Laughing Gas, Viagra, and Lipitor*.

Pfizer. *Phenotypic Drug Discovery Modern Successes*, accessed August 11, 2024.

Swinney, David. "Phenotypic Drug Discovery: History, Evolution, Future." In *Phenotypic Drug Discovery*, edited by Beverley Isherwood and Angelique Augustin, The Royal Society of Chemistry, 2020: 1–19.

Swinney, David, and Jason Anthony. "How Were New Medicines Discovered?" *Nature Reviews Drug Discovery* 10, 7, 2011: 507–519.

Vincent, Fabien, Arsenio Nueda, Jonathan Lee, et al. "Phenotypic Drug Discovery: Recent Successes, Lessons Learned and New Directions." *Nature Reviews Drug Discovery* 21, 12, 2022: 899–914.

Walters, Kevin. *The Invention of Warfarin*, American Chemical Society. 2022.

TDD, SDD, and FXa inhibitors:

Bartfai et al. *Drug Discovery: From Bedside to Wall Street*.

Gossert, Alvar, and Wolfgang Jahnke. "NMR in Drug Discovery: A Practical Guide to Identification and Validation of Ligands Interacting with Biological Macromolecules." *Progress in Nuclear Magnetic Resonance Spectroscopy* 97, 2016: 82–125.

Stockman, Brian. "NMR Spectroscopy as a Tool for Structure-Based Drug Design." *Progress in Nuclear Magnetic Resonance Spectroscopy* 33, 2, August 31, 1998: 109–151.

Computational chemistry, HTS:
Bartusiak, Marcia. "Designing Drugs with Computers." *Discover*, August 1981.
Brown, Frank K., Edward C. Sherer, Scott A. Johnson, M. Katharine Holloway, and Bradley S. Sherborne. "The Evolution of Drug Design at Merck Research Laboratories." *Journal of Computer-Aided Molecular Design* 31, 3, 2017: 255–266.
Leelananda, Sumudu, and Steffen Lindert. "Computational Methods in Drug Discovery." *Beilstein Journal of Organic Chemistry* 12, 2016: 2694–2718.
November, Joseph. *Biomedical Computing*, Johns Hopkins University Press, 2012.
Pollack, Andrew. "Technology: Supercomputers track human genome." *New York Times*, August 28, 2000.

rDNA, XRC, NMR, and other enabling technologies:
Blundell, "Protein Crystallography and Drug Discovery: Recollections of Knowledge Exchange between Academia and Industry."
Blundell, Tom. "A Personal History of Using Crystals and Crystallography to Understand Biology and Advanced Drug Discovery." *Crystals* 10, 8, 2020: 676.
Jaskolski, Mariusz, Zbigniew Dauter, and Alexander Wlodawer. "A Brief History of Macromolecular Crystallography, Illustrated by a Family Tree and Its Nobel Fruits." *The FEBS Journal* 281, 18, 2014: 3985–4009.
Kenney, Martin. *Biotechnology: The University-Industrial Complex*. Yale University Press, 1986.
Petsko, "Dawn of Structural Biology."
Zheng et al., "X-Ray Crystallography."

Table 10

Cytokines (TNF and IL-12/IL23):
Zarros et al., "The Recent History of Tumour Necrosis Factor (TNF)."

Insulin analogs, DPP-4 and SGLT inhibitors:
Ahrén, "DPP-4 Inhibition."
Bliss, *The Discovery of Insulin*.
Cordes, *Hallelujah Moments*.

Stern, Scott. "Incentives and Focus in University and Industrial Research: The Case of Synthetic Insulin." In *Sources of Medical Technology: Universities and Industry*, edited by Nathan Rosenberg, Annetine Gelijns, and Holly Dawkins, National Academy Press, 1995: 157–187.

Direct Factor Xa inhibitors:
Nar, "The Role of Structural Information."
Zheng et al., "Discovery and Development of Factor Xa Inhibitors (2015–2022)."

Table 11

Hughes, *Genentech*.
Li, *Laughing Gas, Viagra, and Lipitor*.
Novo Nordisk. "Insulin 100 Years."
Rasmussen, *Gene Jockeys: Life Science and the Rise of Biotech Enterprise*.
Stern, "Incentives and Focus in University and Industrial Research."

Table 12

Ahrén, "DPP-4 Inhibition."
Cordes, *Hallelujah Moments*.

Table 13

Beitelshees, Amber, Bruce Leslie, and Simeon Taylor. "Sodium–Glucose Cotransporter 2 Inhibitors: A Case Study in Translational Research." *Diabetes* 68, 6, 2019: 1109–1120.
Cordes, *Hallelujah Moments*.
Wright, Ernest, Donald Loo, and Bruce Hirayama. "Biology of Human Sodium Glucose Transporters." *Physiological Reviews* 91, 2, 2011: 733–794.

Table 14

Beutler, Bruce. "TNF (and Its Relatives)." *Parkland Memorial Hospital*, Internal Medicine Grand Rounds, September 26, 1996.
Katz, Robert. "Remembering Etanercept & the Advent of the Biologic Era." *The Rheumatologist*, February 2020.
Love, James. "Federal Support for Research (Enbrel) Etanercept, Evidence from CRISP and Clinicaltrials.Gov." Knowledge Ecology International, November 2, 2009.
Van Loo, Geert, and Mathieu Bertrand. "Death by TNF: A Road to Inflammation." *Nature Reviews Immunology* 23, 5, 2023: 289–303.

Wallach, David. "The Tumor Necrosis Factor Family: Family Conventions and Private Idiosyncrasies." *Cold Spring Harbor Perspectives in Biology* 10, 10, 2018: a028431.

Weinreb, "The Israel inspired revolution in arthritis treatment."

Zarros et al., "The Recent History of Tumour Necrosis Factor (TNF)."

Table 15

Trinchieri, Giorgio. "Interleukin-12 and the Regulation of Innate Resistance and Adaptive Immunity." *Nature Reviews Immunology* 3, 2, 2003: 133–146.

Table 16

Li, Jie. *Blockbuster Drugs: The Rise and Fall of the Pharmaceutical Industry*. Oxford University Press, 2014.

Nar, "The Role of Structural Information in the Discovery of Direct Thrombin and Factor Xa Inhibitors."

Zheng et al., "Discovery and Development of Factor Xa Inhibitors (2015–2022)."

Table 17

Hendriks, Rudi, Saravanan Yuvaraj, and Laurens Kil. "Targeting Bruton's Tyrosine Kinase in B Cell Malignancies." *Nature Reviews Cancer* 14, 4, 2014: 219–232.

Love, James. "KEI Notes on the Clinical Studies for Imbruvica (Ibrutinib)." Knowledge Ecology International, 2023.

Schouten, Arianna. "Notes on the Preclinical Development of Imbruvica (Ibrutinib)." Knowledge Ecology International, 2023.

Shaywitz, David. "The Wild Story behind a Promising Experimental Cancer Drug." *Forbes*, April 5, 2013.

Vardi, Nathan. *For Blood and Money: Billionaires, Biotech, and the Quest for a Blockbuster Drug*. Norton, 2023.

Acknowledgments

Öner Tulum is executive director of research, and William Lazonick, president, of the Academic-Industry Research Network. The authors are grateful to the Institute for New Economic Thinking for funding this project and to INET director of research Thomas Ferguson for his insights into the issues with which this Element is concerned. The Canadian Institute for Advanced Research, Program on Innovation, Equity & the Future of Prosperity has also provided funding for research presented in this Element.

Cambridge Elements

Corporate Governance

Thomas Clarke
UTS Business School, University of Technology Sydney

Thomas Clarke is Professor of Corporate Governance at the UTS Business School of the University of Technology Sydney. His work focuses on the institutional diversity of corporate governance and his most recent book is *International Corporate Governance* (Second Edition 2017). He is interested in questions about the purposes of the corporation, and the convergence of the concerns of corporate governance and corporate sustainability.

About the Series

The series Elements in Corporate Governance focuses on the significant emerging field of corporate governance. Authoritative, lively and compelling analyses include expert surveys of the foundations of the discipline, original insights into controversial debates, frontier developments, and masterclasses on key issues. Its areas of interest include empirical studies of corporate governance in practice, regional institutional diversity, emerging fields, key problems and core theoretical perspectives.

Cambridge Elements⁼

Corporate Governance

Elements in the Series

Value-Creating Boards: Challenges for Future Practice and Research
Morten Huse

Trust, Accountability and Purpose: The Regulation of Corporate Governance
Justin O'Brien

Corporate Governance and Leadership: The Board as the Nexus of Leadership-in-overnance
Monique Cikaliuk, Ljiljana Eraković, Brad Jackson, Chris Noonan and Susan Watson

The Evolution of Corporate Governance
Bob Tricker

Corporate Governance: A Survey
Thomas Clarke

Board Dynamics
Philip Stiles

The Role of the Board in Corporate Purpose and Strategy
Robert Bood, Hans van Ees and Theo Postma

Investing in Innovation: Confronting Predatory Value Extraction in the U.S. Corporation
William Lazonick

The Rhetoric and Reality of Shareholder Democracy and Hedge-Fund Activism
Jan-Sup Shin

Incorporating Purpose: The New Legal Foundations for the Corporation and Its Management
Blanche Segrestin, Kevin Levillain and Armand Hatchuel

Regulating EU Sustainability Reporting: Learning from Failure and Success
David Monciardini

Innovation versus Financialization in the US Pharmaceutical Industry
Öner Tulum and William Lazonick

A full series listing is available at: www.cambridge.org/ECG

For EU product safety concerns, contact us at Calle de José Abascal, 56–1°, 28003 Madrid, Spain or eugpsr@cambridge.org.

www.ingramcontent.com/pod-product-compliance
Lightning Source LLC
LaVergne TN
LVHW011850060526
838200LV00054B/4268